Justice Examined

A Humorous Romp Through the Foibles of the Legal System

Attorney Richard Weiss

authorHOUSE

AuthorHouse™
1663 Liberty Drive, Suite 200
Bloomington, IN 47403
www.authorhouse.com
Phone: 1-800-839-8640

© 2009 Attorney Richard Weiss. All rights reserved.

No part of this book may be reproduced, stored in a retrieval system, or transmitted by any means without the written permission of the author.

First published by AuthorHouse   1/15/2009

ISBN: 978-1-4343-9152-0 (sc)
ISBN: 978-1-4343-9151-3 (hc)

Printed in the United States of America
Bloomington, Indiana

This book is printed on acid-free paper.

"Life is a series of missed opportunities."

I would like to thank the following people who contributed to this book. Andrew Pasquina, Gary Leroy, Earl Miller, Charlotte Creely, Daniel Colatosti, Kathy Centorino and Anne Baum.

Table of Contents

Introduction xi
Priorities 1
Father Knows Best 9
A Man's Home is his Castle 15
The Appeals Court 19
All in the Family 31
The Early Days 33
It's in the Mail 37
Why We Hate Lawyers I 41
The Witness 45
The Oldest Profession 49
In the Parking Lot 55
Closing Argument 57
A Lifetime Job 59
Work Study 65
The Rules 69
Clothes Make the Man 73
No Good Turn Goes Unpunished 77
The Doctor 85
Why We Hate Lawyers II 91
At the Cemetary 95
The Paternity Test 101
A Nice Story 105
What's in a Name 113
The Bill 117
A Gift from God 119

Wedding Night	125
At the Gaming Tables	129
Why We Hate Judges	135
Accident Prone	139
Close to Home	143
Why We Hate Lawyers III	147
The Lottery	151
Precedent	153
The Flood	157
The Beginner	159
The Psychic	163
Public Defending	165
Running the Office I	169
Running the Office II	171
Good News/Bad News	173
What You Don't Know	177
A Restraining Order	179
The Public Service Rule	181
The Translator	185
My Date with Osama	189
You have the Power – Use It Wisely	194
Always Look for a Bargain	196
Second Chance	199
Epilogue	227

INTRODUCTION

The law is everywhere. You know it is working for you when you see the nightly news and police are shown apprehending the criminal "du jour". You also know the law is there when a high profile lawsuit is reported, whether it is a lurid domestic murder case, or some powerful corporation that is being sued for contaminating the environment.

Some say there is too much law. They cite the wisdom of time spent on traffic violations, or apprehending a parolee for purchasing a state sponsored lottery ticket, or the time and energy expended by congress as to whether Roger Clemens took human growth hormones in his tushie, (while a war rages in Iraq).

The above is the high profile news that the general public gets to know about. However, like any discipline, much goes on out of earshot of the public. Most of what transpires follows the high standards that the American legal system is known for. However, in any scenario, that is so important and pervasive in American life, wild stories trickle down and the public is fascinated by them (woman gets one million dollars from McDonalds for spilled cup of coffee).

With any discipline, and with a system that is so integral to American daily life sometimes things occur that might not be construed to the standards of "The Letter of the Law."

I am a practicing attorney in Massachusetts for over thirty years.

I have gathered over forty vignettes that challenge or highlight some of the humorous or bizarre decisions that have been rendered in legal situations that I have been involved with.

I think you will be pleasantly entertained and educated at the human interest stories that I have compiled for your reading entertainment.

Priorities

Background 1:

As most people know from watching television, parties charged with a criminal offense have a constitutional right to be represented in court if the offense carries a period of incarceration if found guilty. New attorneys not blessed with the superstar credentials to be hired by a top law firm, or for that matter more pedestrian attorneys who were unlucky enough not to find any type of employment fresh out of law school, turn to applying to the local courts to be put on a "criminal defense list." These attorneys will be appointed to defend indigents unable to hire an attorney for representation. These appointments run the gamut from assaults, shoplifting, using drugs, driving infractions, to even more serious offenses such as rape and drug dealing.

Background 2:

The Grand Jury

Basically you can become involved in the criminal system in one of several ways. For minor offenses (i.e. punching your neighbor), you apply to the court and a court clerk or a judge will decide whether the complained of action, whether true or not, rises to the level of a criminal act if it were in fact true. If a criminal complaint is issued, the ensuing trial then determines whether the complained of action actually happened. If a judge (or jury) finds the action happened, the person is found guilty. If the tribunal finds the allegation is untrue, the person is found not guilty. For more serious offenses, the criminal act is presented to a group of people, a "Grand Jury", and they similarly decide whether the action itself (not whether the complained of action is true) rises to the level of a criminal act. If the Grand Jury does find that the action constitutes a criminal act, the party is "indicted" and will go through the criminal system. The same outcome as above will also be determined by a trial.

MANDATORY SENTENCING

As you might imagine, since crimes are defined by the legislature, the legislature also prescribes the corresponding punishment for the crime.

Many times a judge will be given discretion to mete out an applicable sentence within the range of sentence parameters. (A rather famous case in Massachusetts was a British nanny who was accused of shaking a baby to death that she was the nanny of. There was a jury trial and the nanny was accused of manslaughter. After trial, a jury found the nanny guilty. The presiding judge did not overturn the jury verdict, but he limited her incarceration to the time served waiting for trial, several hundred days. I guess he felt that she had been punished enough).

One hears a sentence as three to five years, eight to twelve years, even twenty-five years to life. Invariably, eight to twelve years means the party will be eligible for parole around or near the eight-year mark. Even with the above sentences, the judge has the discretion to not even impose any jail time.

Some disgruntled lawmakers wanted to rectify what they felt was too much latitude to criminal judges in meting out sentences.

They created mandatory sentencing. These sentences must be satisfied by a wrongdoer by serving a period of time in jail, recardless of a judge's discretion.

In Massachusetts for instance, if you are carrying a gun that is unlicensed, the mandatory sentencing mandated that you serve a year in jail, with no discretion from the judge to save you.

Violent crimes were not necessarily locked into mandatory sentencing, such as armed robbery. A party could be found guilty of armed robbery, and not even have to do any time. But armed robbery with a mask carried a minimum of a five-year mandatory sentence. Many drug related crimes also have mandatory sentencing.

Like most other things, if you look hard enough you can find a loophole. Mandatory sentencing indeed could not be altered for the specific statute cited, but the court system could circumvent a mandatory sentence by just charging the miscreant with a statute that was similar to the original statute contemplated, but one that did not have mandatory sentencing.

My legal career began with public defending. I would go to court on assigned days and wait to be handed a criminal case.

On this particular day, an eighteen-year-old Irish man was being charged with armed robbery with a mask, a very serious offense. Although I was not that experienced at the time, this did not stop me from accepting the assignment.

Having just turned eighteen, this fellow had a juvenile record. In order to give minors a chance at a fresh start when they turn eighteen, the court system may (but does not have to) seal a person's criminal record. This means the court system cannot use prior offenses to prejudice a person's position in the court system for a current crime. Of course, as you can see, since the cutoff for sealing a record was eighteen years, it did not take long for my client to renew his criminal career.

When I was assigned to the perpetrator, we met after the court allowed him to be on his own and leave the court without setting bail. (He was a veteran of the system, not withstanding his "sealed record", and the court felt comfortable he was not a flight risk.)

In my interview with him, I learned that he had ripped off a fairly well connected drug dealer with a shotgun. He escaped with no money, but a good cache of drugs. His actual offense was "armed robbery with a mask", as he was wearing a mask when he committed the robbery.

In his attempt to set up shop himself and sell the drugs, he obviously wasn't quite as experienced at it as his "victim." He was easily apprehended and the authorities were able to trace back the drugs to the poor "victim." Since the authorities had him dead to rights on the armed robbery, they did not even bother to charge him with selling drugs, the armed robbery being the far more serious offense. He admitted to me that he did do the robbery, and he was rather vague in his strategy for defending himself.

The next order of business was to negotiate with the Assistant District Attorney about a probable cause hearing.

A probable cause hearing is a device where the defense can force a mini hearing that forces the government to reveal the essence of their case against the accused. This allows the defense to learn what they are up against and allows the defendant to defend himself accordingly and as best as he is able.

In wrangling over whether a probable cause hearing will occur, a lot of times "deals" can be made between the defense and the government to suit both sides. The government usually does not like to reveal its case, but of course would have to if no deal can be made.

In this case, the Assistant District Attorney approached me and said if I waived the probable caused hearing, when the Assistant District

Attorney presented his case to the Grand Jury, he would omit the part "with a mask."

This was quite significant because the law has different levels of punishment for different crimes. You could attack people, steal, sell drugs, even rape, and under certain circumstances be convicted of the crime but not necessarily do time. However, the controlling statute in my case made armed robbery WITH A MASK, have a mandatory punishment of serving a minimum of five years in prison. This was significant because it would seem that if my fellow was found guilty, which seemed likely, I would have no wiggle room to keep him out of jail.

I agreed to the Assistant DA's offer. I thought I was making progress.

Several weeks later, I was informed by the Assistant District Attorney that my fellow was indeed indicted for armed robbery, but also "with a mask". I asked the Assistant District Attorney what about the deal that we had made. He replied that he had reported the facts of the robbery to the Grand Jury, and it was they, the grand jury, who had indicted my client "with a mask". Obviously, the D.A. could have presented the facts to the Grand Jury and omitted the facts "with a mask." It was a serious lesson for a young attorney and an insight into the zealousness of my adversaries, even to the extent that the assistant district attorney would prostitute himself and lie to me to gain any advantage, even at the cost of his word. I was now saddled with defending my client with a mandatory prison sentence hanging over his head.

My next move found me rather than me finding it. The investigating detective approached me at the pre-trial hearing and said to me "The kid is not really a bad kid. He's been on the street all his life and he knows a lot of names and what's going down. If he comes to me and gives me some names of heavy hitters, I will go to bat for him at the trial."

I did not know what "going to bat for the kid" exactly entailed, but I was sure it must be better than going it alone and facing the mandatory charges of going to jail. Also, since my client actually was guilty, help from any quarter was welcome.

I approached my client with the detective's offer, and he was only lukewarm with it at best. I know there is a code on the street about "snitching" but there also is the concept of self-preservation, and the kid needed to be taken by the shoulders and given a good shaking. However, it was not going to be me!

The time between the pretrial, where my conversation with the detective occurred, and the trial, was several months. I parted ways with my client with the promise that he would indeed approach our "friendly" detective.

The fateful Monday arrived and I was in court at 9:00 o'clock. My client soon arrived and I went out of the courtroom to meet him. I asked him, "so you met with the detective, didn't you?" Much to my amazement, his response was no. Incredulously, I asked him "Why not?" His answer was simple and to the point. "I WAS BUSY."

Perhaps various people have a guardian angel. In this case, my rather profligate client did seem blessed. On this day, a judge in the judicial system had passed away, and all cases were postponed! They rescheduled us for the following Thursday.

As we walked out of court, I approached my client and asked if he thought he could find some time to meet with the detective. He said he would see what he could do.

Thursday rolled around and we reassembled at court. "Did you see the Detective?" I asked. Since I now did not know what to expect, his affirmative response really gave me a sigh of relief, though my client still seemed unimpressed by the whole detective thing.

I approached the Detective and he did confirm that my client gave him enough information that he was satisfied that my client "did his duty" and he would indeed go to bat for him. Going to bat for him, in this case meant that the court would find him guilty of the crime, but he would not have to do jail time. I was so euphoric that I was accomplishing my job that I forgot about the mandatory aspect of the crime.

Court was called and our case was first. The Judge asked if we wanted to have a meeting in chambers, and of course, I very much wanted to have a meeting in chambers.

We assembled in chambers, the Assistant District Attorney, the Detective, the Judge, and me. There is small talk, and what I found interesting was the fact that everybody was Irish, except me, of course. After all, I was practicing in Massachusetts!

As this low level banter continued, I meekly spoke up and, directing my question to the judge, "Can I ask a question?"

"Sure son," was the judges response "Well, the Detective said my client would not have to go to jail if he cooperated, but I don't see how that can happen if armed robbery with a mask has a mandatory sentencing of five years." "Son", the judge bellowed, "I can do anything that I want."

And so he did! My client was convicted of armed robbery (with a mask was finally mysteriously omitted) and he did not have to serve any time.

It would be nice to say that my client used this rather lucky turn of events as a springboard to become an esteemed member of society. However, real life does not work that way. Several months later, my young man called me to inquire about representing him for an attempted rape. I was game, but I never did hear from him again.

Father Knows Best

Background:

In most situations, a person using the court system for redress has the choice of going before a judge or jury. (Certain actions, such as probate matters, divorce, child custody, etc. only allow a trial with a judge). However, the system directs that in a situation, such as a regular automobile accident, you can have the hearing either by judge or jury. If you want a trial by a judge, both parties have to agree on that. If one of the participants demands that they want a jury to decide an action, that decision predominates over their counterpart who might have been content with having their case heard only by a judge. A trial by judge is much simpler and goes far more quickly than a trial by jury. With a jury, procedures have to be handled with kid gloves. The jury can only be exposed to what is considered proper evidence. Therefore, the jury is continually sheltered while the opposing lawyers bicker over the management of the case.

A married couple, approximately in their early forties, came to me with the following problem. They were a middle class family, with several children, who had minor savings and were living basically from paycheck to paycheck. They were not in financial distress, but they were not close, for instance, to being able to purchase their own home.

The wife had both a widowed mother and a sister. The mother had been living with her daughter (my client's sister) and obviously had a closer relationship with that daughter than my client.

Mother had contacted her other daughter (my client) and had made her the following proposition. Mother had savings and she had found a house for sale that she thought would suit her and her family, her two daughters. It was a two family home with an in-law apartment, in the basement. She invited my client to move in the house together with her and her other sister. Each sister would take a floor. The mother would even live in the basement! Further, she stated that they would all live together, and ultimately she would leave the house to her two daughters. My clients mulled over the proposition and ultimately accepted it.

It should be noted that in many situations such as this, transactions by and between close family members, there was no written contract between the participants. This means that significant things might not have occurred. First, since there was nothing written, a true meeting of the minds might not have been accomplished. Perhaps the actual understanding was not the same understanding by each party. Second, with nothing written, if there was going to be trouble in paradise, everybody's rights might not be protected. I am sure, if any party had even suggested that the arrangement be written, this might have offended both of the other parties. After all, what is closer than the mother/daughter bond?

Mother purchased the home of her dreams, and both sisters moved in as per the arrangement. Each sister paid their proportionate share of the costs of living in the home, including a portion of the mortgage, utilities, repairs, etc. Basically, everybody got along as per their verbal arrangement.

My clients did more than honor their arrangement with mother. The husband began to treat the property as his own, and why shouldn't

Justice Examined

he? He cheerfully did basic maintenance around the house. He mowed the lawn, shoveled snow, cleared the common areas.

In fact, the husband paved the driveway and installed a flagpole on the property. Who installs a flagpole at the place where he is living that does not feel the property that they are dealing with will indeed be their own some day in the future?

The next step is harder to reconcile. Literally, virtually in the middle of the night, mother sold the property, leaving my clients to be subject of the wrath of the new owners who immediately began eviction proceedings.

Mother and her other daughter settled comfortably into a single family home with an in-law apartment (naturally), with no explanation to my clients, and certainly no monetary recompense to my clients. However, far more damaging to my clients was the fact that the mother now reneged on her verbal arrangement to ultimately give half the house to my clients.

I get the "story" from my clients and it is only human nature for them to put on a positive "spin" on the story to bolster their own position. I am sure that it was not a paradise living in the old house, but still, a deal is a deal.

So my clients come to me and ask if they have any rights under these circumstances, and I inform them that they do.

Background 2:

In most jurisdictions, if one wants to enforce a verbal promise, they are legally denied that right because the promise was not put in writing. This is especially true when promises are made to leave you something by will if you render services to that person while they are alive. Invariably, the promising party dies and has failed in their promise to leave the person rendering services to the deceased anything by will. When this happens, you are prevented from legally attacking the deceased person, but the law does allow you an "end run". You are allowed to sue the deceased person's estate for "services rendered." You are allowed to convince a jury that you should be reimbursed for all the work you were induced to do by the deceased, but now find yourself uncompensated for. This scenario is called suing for "services rendered" and is quite popular in the legal community for attacking the many promises that are made by elder family members to induce their younger relatives to assist them with the promise of a payoff at death. However, a less common scenario was this one, where the promissor was still alive, but the concept was the same.

I informed my clients that the way to attack this situation (and her mother), was to sue for services rendered. The fact pattern was similar even though the mother was still alive. The daughter, my client, would say she was induced to render services with the payoff being the ownership of the mother's home. Since the mother was reneging on her promise, we would be allowed to attack her collaterally for her promises that went unfulfilled. After all, my clients had such evidence as the aforementioned flagpole and paved driveway. Also, both sides agreed to have a trial by judge, rather than a trial by jury.

In bringing a lawsuit, you start by filing a formal written complaint. One lists a series of statements in paragraph form, outlining what you feel the wronged action has been by the other side. My main paragraph stated:

Defendant (Mother) induced Plaintiff (my client) to perform services with no intention of compensating her for the services so rendered. The complaint had many other paragraphs outlining my client's situation (we lawyers are very verbal), but the above reflects the essence of the complaint.

Justice Examined

Trial day arrived. I, as plaintiff's attorney, present my case through the testimony of my clients (and other witnesses, if appropriate). The defense acts similarly.

We are allowed to cross-examine each other's witnesses. When mother was put on the stand, who was about 70 and partially blind, I cross-examined.

I am not the next coming of Perry Mason. I do my best.

One of the tacks that I chose to use was as follows:

Me: "Do you love your daughters equally?"
Mother: "Yes"
Me: "Did you want your daughters to live with you?"
Mother: "Yes"
Me: "Did you ask your daughters to help you around the house?"
Mother: "Yes"
Me: "Did you want to hurt your daughter for something she did to you?"
Mother: "Absolutely not. I love both of my daughters."

At some point my questions must have hit a nerve, because mother finally blurts out: "I love my daughter. I asked her to come live with me and I would give her my house if she came and lived with me. I wanted to keep my girls together. I love them both."

Well, I was a young, somewhat inexperienced attorney at the time, but I knew when I hit a homerun. Mother had essentially blurted out the essence of my client's claim against her mother as I had outlined it in my complaint. It doesn't get any better than that if you are litigating a case.

I quickly stopped my cross examination (where could I go?) and wound up my case. The trial was over (almost).

Attorney Richard Weiss

Cases have final summations where the attorney summarizes what he or she feels are the main points of their case.

Let me comment upon the judge that was presiding over the case. He was about sixty-five and a person I speculated to be very conservative. Throughout the trial, I sensed that he felt that suing one's mother was not the correct thing to do. Nevertheless, he was the judge I was dealt, so I had little choice but to proceed and attempt to appease him and persuade him that our side was the right side.

I am doing my summation and I sensed it was not going that well. In the middle of my spiel, I said: "You know, your honor, Mother admitted exactly what I had stated in my complaint, almost word for word."

Much to my amazement the judge snarls back "Yeah, that's the best part of your case." When he said that, I knew we were in trouble.

In due course, the judge rendered his decision, and I am sure you can tell that it was against my clients.

A judge, in most situations, has to justify his findings based on the evidence that has been presented and his impressions and such that he has drawn from the testimony.

Not to be remiss in documenting his judgment (and for a better chance for the decision to stand up if an appeal is taken) the judge did address the mother's admission with:

"I know your mother made the statement that she induced your client to come live with her BUT SHE DIDN'T MEAN IT."

Just like that, after two years of preparing the case, after getting the mother to essentially admit the allegations against her, the judge has the power to render a decision on what he feels is the greater and justifiable "right" (don't sue your mother!). Doesn't seem fair!

A Man's Home is his Castle

Background:

It has been determined (through case law) that a homeowner can use sufficient force to protect himself and the sanctity of his home. Therefore, when the threat to the homeowner at his home is proportionately more dangerous, the homeowner would be allowed to use more force. If the situation threatened the life of the homeowner, and the homeowner reasonably thought that that was the case, then the homeowner would be justified in using deadly force to protect himself. Sometimes, a homeowner might very well decide that deadly force was necessary in his time of distress, and the authorities might decide otherwise. A criminal action might be commenced if such a divergent point of view arose.

A forty-ish year old client comes to my office to discuss his bankruptcy. As many times happens, he brings a family member that would like to discuss a problem that has arisen in his life. I am more than happy to accommodate requests such as this. You never know when a meeting like this will generate more business.

The gentleman is his uncle, let's call him Tim, who, I find out, is sixty-two years old. This occurred twenty years ago, and that era's sixty year olds were still squarely ensconced as sixty year olds. He was quite old fashioned and showed his age.

He had married late in life, and he appeared to be insanely jealous of his wife. As the questioning played out, it rose to the fact that he was absolutely convinced that his wife was cheating on him. When I inquired as to how he had come to this conclusion, it became evident that he had no actual proof of his wife's supposed infidelities. "I have seen footprints in the snow" was his best attempt at an accusation. Nevertheless, he was adamant that she was cheating.

After he had painfully made his point, we spent some time going over the basic ground rules of divorce. In this case, because it was a marriage late in life, and there were no children, the intricacies of a divorce, ranging from custody, visitation and child support, were not relevant.

The second most important topic we touched upon was division of assets. Obviously, this is also of paramount importance, as it can lead people to contemplate, and sometimes implement, drastic measures between the parties.

Also, in a marriage of shorter duration, the assets that one party brings into the marriage do not necessarily get shared by the other party. My new possible client had only been married for four years.

The entirety of this informational discussion was force fed into my hoped to be new client, but I could see that his understanding, and more importantly, his heart, was not into it. His best retorts were the footprints in the snow, mentioned frequently and building fervor.

I was hitting him with my best presentation, but I was still not holding his interest.

Finally, he meekly interrupted me and asked me if I would answer a question for him. I said of course.

He reiterated that in spite of all my assurances that she was probably not cheating on him, and the fact that he had no concrete proof that she was cheating, he knew in his heart that she was not pure.

"Let me ask you" he said. "Would it be all right if one day after I had left our home for work, if I snuck back into the house, took my shotgun and hid in the cellar? If my wife came home with another man, I could jump out and blow both of them away!"

At this point bells and whistles started going off in my head. Sometimes, one might not clearly think in a stressful situation. However, I was right on this! I know that now was not the time to be sarcastic and come out with a flip "oh sure, no problem, if you saw that, you'd have every right to blow her away." Now was not the time to test his sense of irony or sarcasm if I made such a statement.

I envisioned the news blurb "man shoots wife with his attorney's permission – details at eleven."

I pictured the eleven o'clock news. Cameras swarming outside of a house; a man shackled, agitated, one of those reporters shoves a microphone in the man's face "Why did you shoot your wife?"

"I caught the whore cheating on me; my lawyer said it was all right to shoot her if I caught her in the act!"

I figured I might have a hard time explaining my advice to the bar regulators, the attorney's watchdog agency that governs the ethics that the lawyers have to follow. Even with my comic timing, sense of irony and deadpan delivery, the explanation of why I told my client he could shoot his no good two timing whore of a wife would just be too hard!

"NO. TIM THAT WOULD NOT BE ALL RIGHT. IF THAT HAPPENS, IF YOU CATCH HER IN THE ACT, JUST CALL THE POLICE."

The Appeals Court

Background:

The appeal process is misunderstood by the average person. An appeal of a legal decision might exist as a matter of right, but to implement the appeal, the appeal should be based on a presumed error that was made at the trial level. There will always be abuses as there is in every facet of life, but it should be understood that to appeal a decision (that is not a murder case), the appellants (the side appealing) ostensibly are challenging a legal decision that was made by the judge during trial. For instance, one side might have thought that it was appropriate for a psychiatrist to testify to the proclivities of a person at trial, but the judge would not allow the psychiatrist to testify on the subject. The decision of the judge would be the type of possible error that would be correctly appealable. That is, if the appeals court agreed, they would rule that the judge made an error in denying the psychiatrist to testify. The appeals court would then have grounds to order a new trial.

There are two additions to the concept of appeal. The first is that any aggrieved party who has lost a trial can appeal that the decision is "against the weight of the evidence." As you can imagine, this is the catchall, kitchen sink type reason for an appeal utilized by a desperate party, when they have nothing else to hang their hat on, and this concept is greatly overused. The second exception is that in all murder cases, if the defendant is convicted of the murder, the appeal of the case is done automatically. (In Massachusetts, at least.)

The second overall concept that governs appeals is that the appeals court has to be strictly bound by what is before them. What I mean by this is that at a trial, not only does the judge or jury make their decision on the facts that they hear, but they are allowed, even encouraged, to judge and weigh the demeanor of the parties testifying, and make their decision based on those intangibles, as well as the facts testified to. The appeals court does not have the luxury of getting a bad taste in their mouth about a party, and rule against them because of that intangible feeling. The appeal judges are bound only by what is before them with the written word.

A woman comes to my office knee deep in a medical malpractice appeal. Her underlying case was that her daughter was allegedly injured in childbirth. The birth had been difficult, and the doctors had resorted to forceps to assist in the birth. Supposedly, the forceps were mishandled, and the doctors injured the baby's head while trying to extract the baby from the mother's womb.

The mother had also been roughed up in the birthing process. What this means is that when a lawyer is forced to bring a lawsuit (as opposed to settling the case without the necessity of a trial) the lawyer, in bringing a complaint, will "throw in the kitchen sink". It essentially does not cost more, nor does it dilute the main thrust of action (as in this case the damage to the child was much more the important case). You never know, if the trial goes well and the jury comes to dislike the defendant doctor, the jury could decide to punish the doctor by not only a big judgment for the baby, but a second big judgment on behalf of the mother.

In this case, the mother had been offered a one hundred thousand dollar settlement, but she refused it as not being adequate for the damage she thought her daughter had suffered. Her lawyer, in this case, had encouraged her to accept the offer, citing the complexities of the case and that the one hundred thousand dollars was fair because of all the intangibles in the case.

The mother would have none of this. Sometimes, a person in the mother's position understands more about the case then even her lawyer. She has "lived" not only the trauma of the malpractice, but she also had been there for every facet of the preparation of the case, and she certainly grasped more than a mere cursory overview of the case.

That might be the good news for the intervention of the mother in this case. The bad news is that the mother is not an attorney, does not understand all the subtleties of doing a trial, does not understand to what facts will instill negative ideas impacting on how a jury will react to the case, not be quite so empathetic to the injuries that her little girl had suffered, and a whole host of other intangibles that might have been brought out at the trial.

In any event, the mother did reject the one hundred thousand dollar offer and the parties proceeded to trial.

After that part of the trial where both sides put in their evidence to convince the jury that their side is the righteous side, a judge addresses the jury, explaining the law that is appropriate in the type of case the jury has heard, and how to apply that law to the facts of the case that the jury has heard. If the case is simple, for instance did the defendant go through a red light or not, you can imagine that the judge's explanation to the jury is relatively simple. If the trial is complicated, if there are multiple issues, if there are multiple plaintiffs, if there is certain law that pertains to one plaintiff, but not the other, all types of things that may occur and did occur in a trial such as this, then you can imagine that when the judge addresses the jury to explain everything, his "charge", as it is called, is much more complicated.

After the judge's charge, the jury duly deliberated and decided against the mother and her daughter.

After the Plaintiff lost, the plaintiff's team had to regroup and decide whether anything that occurred during the trial was either plainly wrong, or any decisions made by the judge were done significantly incorrectly so that by implementing the opposite position, would actually cause the finding of the jury to be changed.

You can always find rulings at a trial that you do not like. But do they rise to the level of changing the outcome of the case? Usually not. This latter concept is called materiality. Sometimes, there can be an acknowledged error, but if it is not material, if the changing of what was complained of would not have changed the jury's decision, then that error by the judge will not cause the appeals court to order a new trial. The name for this is harmless error.

Let me now explain what jury instructions are. When a case is complicated such as this one was, the jury might be called upon to make various decisions. In this case, the jury might find that the doctor was negligent as to the baby, but was not negligent with respect to the mother.

In order to accommodate all these possibilities, the judge formulates a series of questions called jury questions:

Was the doctor negligent with respect to the mother? If so go to the second question. If the doctor was negligent to the child, but not to the mother, go to question three.

The next question might probably say "Determine in dollars the extent of the damage caused to the mother. Question four would address the damages to the baby, and so fourth.

The judge formulates these questions and then invites the opposing attorneys to examine the questions, make suggestions and objections, and puts the questions in a form that is satisfactory to both sides.

This question form would be then submitted to the jury for their determination. These questions become blueprints that allows the jury to navigate through the decision making process.

Here the judge formulated the first question as follows:

"Do you find that the doctor was negligent to BOTH the mother and the child? If you do, go on to question 2. If you do not so find, the case is over.

The jury determined that the doctor was not negligent to both mother and child, and they so indicated in their finding. So the case was over.

You can see what happened here. The first question combined the mother's damages with the child's damages. The case did not have to be approached this way. While the suit could be brought by both mother and daughter, the decisions could and should be rendered separately. The first question inextricably linked the mother's damages and the baby's problems.

Sometimes an error is considered "harmless error". That is, there will be an acknowledged error, but the appeals court will determine that even though the judge had acted incorrectly, the error would not have been significant enough to actually change the outcome of the case.

This error certainly seems like it was more than "harmless error."

An appeal must be filed within thirty days of the finding of the court. The mother, who was on limited means, was unable to employ a lawyer for the appeal, filed the appeal herself. Her lawyer, whom on the one hand had fought valiantly for her rights, and obtained a one hundred thousand dollar offer, now abandoned her on the appeal.

Necessity is the mother of invention. The mother had to learn how to file the appeal, and learn the rules she did!

She had performed the necessary steps to process the appeal to the point that she had come to me. The next step in the appeal process was to write a brief, supporting the mother's position on whatever issue she was appealing. In this case, her main thrust was of the first question linking the damages of both the mother and daughter together.

When she came to me, we sat down for a long time going over the whole trial, the preparation leading up to it, what transpired at trial, the offer of one hundred thousand dollars and of course, the formulation of the special jury questions (as they are called).

Much to my delight, and unfortunately my client's horror, I told her she had a good case, but not in the way that she thought.

I first told her that when doing a pure appeal under all circumstances you start with almost having two feet in the grave. As you can imagine, if the structure were such that most appeals were successful, the trial system would be in chaos. (This is so because if appeals were routinely successful, the cases in the legal system would almost double. Every adverse decision causing disgruntled clients would mean that the disgruntled clients would appeal and have a good shot at causing a new trial. The system can hardly handle the number of cases that are filed yearly, let alone having the courts to readdress the same case over again.)

So then what was I so enthusiastic about? I directed her attention to the first special question. That question was conceived by the judge, but then allowed to stand by her own attorney. (Of course, the opposing attorney was tickled pink to allow the poorly phrased question to stand.)

I told my new client that the focus of her case should be on the malpractice of her attorney! I explained to her the structure of creating jury questions. The judge formulates the questions. He then invites the attorneys to comment and correct the questions to their proper form. Therefore, it is actually a joint effort between judge and attorneys to come up with appropriate questions that will accomplish what the questions are supposed to do, give the jury a road map to "solve" the jury verdict.

Therefore, an error in the jury question ultimately falls on the attorney's shoulders if they are improper. Her attorney had the opportunity to object to this question, and he missed it. Yes, it was true that the judge was also negligent in formulating the question in that way. However, the structure of the trial is such that the attorneys are invited to participate in the formulation of the special questions, and thus the ultimate burden falls upon the attorneys to present appropriate questions to the jury. If a question is presented to the jury at the insistence of the judge, and the lawyer objects at that time, and if the attorney is correct, that would be the issue that the appeal is based. Presumably, in this case, had my new client's attorney objected to the first question in the way it was presented, the judge would have revised his approach and made two questions that recognized that the negligence of the doctor could have been separated between the mother and daughter. My client was attentive as I explained how the creation of the jury question came about, but she did not want to abandon her appeal!

Could the appeals court grant a new trial on this error? I did not think so. I felt the appeals court would "pass the buck" just as I have outlined it here, and would have concluded that it was ultimately not on the shoulder's of the judge, but the obligation of the plaintiff's attorney to get the questions right.

When you have your life's work (almost) in the palm of your hands, you are reluctant to simply abandon all you have worked for and throw it away.

This is also not to mention that this woman had just literally been screwed by her very prestigious first attorney in making such a bonehead error, and now I was asking her, a relative neophyte in the high stakes game of medical malpractice, to simply abandon the appeal, and start on a different tack, a legal malpractice case against her very highly respected attorney.

She asked me if we could proceed with the appeal and simultaneously file a lawsuit against the attorney. I did not think this would click. I told her I believed we would have to allow this appeal to run its course, and then, if I were correct about the appeal decision (and it was dismissed), then attack her previous attorney for legal malpractice for allowing the ambiguous question to be put to the jury.

This answer perked up my client. It was clear she was never going to abandon her appeal.

In spite of my opinion, and my bringing in several other attorneys to back up my opinion, there was just no way my client was going to say yes Mr. Weiss, you are so wise and I am comfortable in abandoning what I thought I was fighting for my baby, and take your advice, as against the reputation of the most highly thought of attorney in the city.

Of course, you might think, what's the problem? The question as formulated was so improper and incorrect, that one way or another, my client should be vindicated on appeal. Also, as I have said, I felt the Appeals Court would only address the jury questions and nothing more, thus rendering the Appeals Court involvement moot.

Appeals Courts are notorious for sneaking out the back door. What I mean by this is that a case with a whole host of factors is presented to the Appeals Court. Even if the case presents a burning issue, if a lesser problem sabotages the issue from being presented to the Appeal Court, the court may decline to address that main issue because the presentation was poisoned by lesser problems that does not allow the court to address the main issue, or at least gives the appeals court the excuse not to address the main point.

For instance, most people know what Roe v. Wade stands for. However, when the actual case was heard by the Supreme Court, the woman had had her child. In this case, the court decided that the abortion issue was so important for the country that they decided to address it. However, on another day, if the court was out of sorts, they might very well have deferred the issue of abortion because in the Roe v. Wade case, the issue became moot because of the birth of the child. I was confident that the court would shoot down the appeal for the reasons I have stated, and that they would then conclude they did not have to address the actual issue of whether the first question was defective because the first ruling would have disposed of the appeal.

However as Robert Burns was heard to say, the best laid plans of mice and men often go astray!

I dutifully wrote the brief for my client. I pointed out the error of the judge. I did not dwell on the fact that the lawyer was the person responsible for the error – let the Appeals Court figure that out itself.

Appeals grind exceedingly slowly, and we anxiously waited for the decision.

Finally, the decision came down. Just as I predicted, the court denied the appeal for the reasons I have stated. They carefully explained that it was the obligation of the attorney, and not the judge to make sure that the questions were presented in proper form.

As I read the Appeals Court finding, I was actually lulled into a false sense of security. Surely, the Appeals Court would not go farther in their finding, content that they disposed of the Appeal accurately and correctly. (And of course, there was no question in my mind that the actual allowance of the poorly phrased first question was indeed malpractice – against my client's first attorney.)

Remember what I said at the beginning of this chapter. The Appeals Court has to operate within the strict purview of what is put before them. What the Appeals Court had here was that the horrendous first question that clearly "married" the fate of the mother's damages with the damages of the child. Sort of like a two for one special. It was almost like saying that for the Plaintiffs to recover, both Plaintiffs had to be injured by the doctor and of course, no such connection was required or demanded by either the court system, or even the appeals court.

Given this foundation, how was the Appeals Court going to screw my client?

Every case has a "charge", a thirty to sixty minute speech by the judge to the jury to spell out the law and what the jury's duty is. Obviously, the judge touches on all relevant points and law.

The Appeals Court did something I had never seen done prior to that point or since. The Appeals Court said that even though they did not have to, they would address the issue of the wayward question.

The Appeals Court said that the question put to the jury was sufficient BECAUSE THE JURY WOULD HAVE UNDERSTOOD WHAT THE JUDGE MEANT.

I have been on several juries and spoken with jurors from other cases. The one thing that I have learned is that except for social misfits, professional liars, or misogynists, people put in a position of authority and charged with meting out decisions in a correct manner, these people will bend over backwards to do their job correctly. In the absence of some corrective statement by the judge, it is hard to see how the jury could ever have "understood what the judge meant" with such an explicit and clear directive as stated in that first jury question. I actually believe that the appeals court went that "extra mile" as a courtesy to my client's first attorney. He was a prestigious attorney from a prestigious law firm. I do not see how it could be anything else but that.

It was all downhill from here. My client wanted to push on with the case, but the Appeal Court's finding essentially exonerated my client's previous attorney. If we had withdrawn the appeal, the Appeals Court would never have had the opportunity to address this issue. I feel confident that this error by her previous attorney would have been fatal to him. A second jury would not have found that the jury "would have understood what the Judge meant."

As it was, my client had made two tremendous errors in judgment that ultimately cost her the vindication and money that she was seeking for the birth doctor's negligence.

Unfortunately, the mother's zeal to get a satisfactory money judgment, and her truculence and stubbornness in not listening to her lawyers, her expert first lawyer, to take the one hundred thousand dollars, and myself to abandon her appeal, cost her the crusade, and unfortunately it ultimately cost her wronged baby the vindication of a fair money judgment.

All in the Family

Background:

An arraignment is the process where a party is charged openly in court with the crime that he is accused of committing. While many career criminals will waive the reading of the precise particulars of the statute that outlines the elements of the crime that one is accused of, sometimes the explanation of the crime will be read. The concept of the arraignment is extremely important in as much as this is one of the cornerstones of democracy. This is as opposed to Fascist regimes (or worse) where there is always the threat that a public citizen will be detained by secret hit squads and his supposed crime will not be aired publicly to prevent that the party will not be railroaded in the system or worse, that in more severe regimes, the party may disappear altogether. With no arraignments, our court system would be a scary, dangerous place.

Representing a client accused driving under the influence of alcohol, I find myself at a District Court. The structure of the court system is that the court clerk usually "Calls the list" to let you know the court has not forgotten to schedule you for your listed appearance, and conversely to make sure the defendants are in attendance in court. The court system usually addresses the new cases first, and the arraignment is the first step in a criminal case.

Attorney Richard Weiss

The lawyers usually are together sitting near the front of the court. Accused felons and miscreants, as well as the visitors of the felons-to-be, sit in the gallery, waiting to be integrated in the criminal treadmill.

Case after case is called and the corresponding accused respond by going to the front of the court, with their attorneys, if they have secured one. The more experienced veterans, who know the script, respond that they are here when their case is called. They are either arraigned, or waive the actual reading of the complaint, get assigned a second date for a "pretrial" and are dismissed from court (if the crime is not so serious that the court would want bail). If the judge deems that the offense is serious enough, and the person might be a flight risk, it is at this point that the issue of bail would be addressed.

As you can imagine, the new crop of criminals are a motley group. Usually they are dressed in casual clothes that look like they have been dredged up from the bottom of the hamper.

After running through half the list, the clerk calls John Baker. A person probably sixty years old effortlessly appears dressed in an expensive suit with an equally expensive lawyer. He is accused of passing bad checks, forging several people's names on some checks and kiting checks (trying to manipulate check writing among several accounts with only one basic sum of money). Most of the attorneys who have been casually watching proceeding, do not think too much of this. However, the clerk next calls Thomas Baker and starts reading off his offenses, which are surprisingly similar to John Baker. This gentleman seems to be about thirty-five with a strong resemblance to the previous seen John Baker.

Without missing a beat, all the attorneys clustered in their area turn to each other and begin smirking and making small asides.

We all agreed that it was nice to see a father take the time to teach his son the family business.

The Early Days

Background:

Bankruptcy is a unique and powerful concept. It allows a person who has not defrauded anybody, and does not owe taxes or educational loans, to simply declare all their other debts null and void. The concept of Bankruptcy was created to allow the party to get "a new start in life." This is assuming you do not have any other significant assets to offset your liabilities. If you do have assets, they must be used to satisfy all of your debts. So bankruptcy becomes a good news/bad news type situation where you might be able to start over and have a fresh start, but, of course, your start basically with just your underwear.

Everybody goes through life in their own way. Conventional people are orderly, accept most of what they see and learn, and try to make sense out of what is going on around them.

More analytical people are constantly amazed at what they find out. They are always weighing the facts that they learn and become continually amazed at the seemingly myriad of little coincidences that occur each day. Sometimes, this over analyzation will bog down a person's rational thinking to the extent that he might not be able to see "the forest because the trees are in the way".

We all have our crosses to bear!

Attorney Richard Weiss

A gay female comes to me for a bankruptcy. Her circumstances were that she had started a company with her soon to be life partner. The business at first was gangbusters.

While things were firing on all cylinders, she and her partner decided to "marry". This was way before the landmark legislation of Massachusetts (that allowed gay marriages). These ladies were not in your face liberals who wanted to confront every disapproving person, but they also were not ashamed of their sexuality and wanted to take their situation one step further to memorialize their relationship, and their devotion to each other.

Both had names like Greenburg and Boardman. They decided to change both their names to Greenboard, a little strange sounding, but certainly doing the trick of cementing their bond, and giving each equal emotional footing in their relationship.

While they were together, they were a happy and successful couple. However, their business took a turn for the worse, and with that, their relationship began to deteriorate. Ultimately, they decided to split up. I did not learn whether my client's partner had changed her name back to her original name, but my client kept the name "Greenboard".

When you go into bankruptcy, you file a petition with the Federal government listing all your creditors that you would like to eliminate. At the time that Ms. Greenboard filed bankruptcy, the Federal Court assigned a "Trustee", a lawyer who represented the interests of the Federal Government. It was his job to make sure the bankruptcy was prepared properly. The trustee had to make sure that the petitioner, called the debtor, was not abusing the process, and all creditors were duly given notice of the debtor's intent.

As luck would have it, the lawyer who was assigned to this case was an acquaintance of mine. For lack of a more genteel way of describing us, we both were into the mathematical side of life. Some would call this gambling, I preferred to characterize it as a person who liked to take calculated risks.

I had met the Trustee while occasionally frequenting the track. We both approached life by weighing mathematically everything that happened to us on a daily basis. You could say that we were both anal in our daily assessment of life's daily peculiarities.

My client and I had missed our first meeting with the Trustee at the courthouse and had to set up a second meeting at his office.

On the appointed day, my client and I come to his office. We had some small talk and then the trustee went about his business of "examining" my client. To do a bankruptcy, the debtor fills out an elaborate petition. The petition tries to be comprehensive concerning anything to do with money. Not only are questions asked such as how much do you have in your bank account, what property you own, what cars you have, but the bankruptcy asks more probing questions such as whether you have owned real property in the last few years or if you are holding property for another person (This question is asked as a defense against fraud.)

As the questions were asked, they were answered easily by my client. After all, she had nothing to hide and was anxious to get this mini-inquisition over.

Then the trustee came to the question "Have you been in business with any other person in the last year?" My client casually answered "yes".

"Who was that person," the trustee innocently asked.

"Patricia Greenboard," the answer.

"Oh," the trustee said, "is that your sister?"

"No" was the answer.

"Your mother", the trustee pressed on, but very innocently, no suspicions.

"No" the same answer.

At this point, the trustee, my gambling buddy from the track, goes ballistic. He says to my client, "Your business partner is not related to you"

My client, as naturally as possible responds "No"

The trustee is now jumping around and virtually in awe of this woman. He gathers his equanimity as best as he is able. He realizes he is supposed to be conducting an examination, but he has the uncontrolled demeanor of a slot player just hitting a giant jackpot. He responds:

"I can't believe it," he is now almost uncontrollable. I'm forty-seven years old and I never even heard of this name, let alone met someone with that name. And not only do you meet someone, you actually go into business with her".

As a risk taker (read: gambler), I know what's running through his mind. He is marveling on the odds of something like this happening, and he can't believe it. Too bad it's not something I can translate to some positive money making scheme, but at least the trustee is enjoying himself while reveling and marveling at the impossibility of this coincidence happening.

As the trustee can't be consoled and is still in amazement at the odds of this happening, I finally interject "Let's move on" "we have to get going". The trustee, still flustered, reluctantly continues with his examination. He was talking to himself as we parted ways.

He probably still stays up late at night marveling at the coincidence that befell my client – unless he finally figured it out.

It's in the Mail

In the eighties, relatively early in my career, a lawyer for a prestigious law firm called me. She explained that she had a cousin that was in her fifties and frankly, she was a pain in the ass. She was mentally ill and she haunted that lawyer's law firm. Her father had previously died and established a small trust fund that hopefully would last through the woman's lifetime.

It was awkward for the law firm and the cousin to accommodate this woman, and she asked if I would take her on, be her trustee. There would probably be up to twenty thousand dollars in administrative fees over her life span. I, being relatively new to the game, was seduced by that twenty thousand dollar prediction.

I met with my new client and we hit it off pretty well. She was a smart lady, notwithstanding her mental illness. In the seventies, she was clear-headed enough to have worked at a stock brokerage firm for a period of time.

My new client came with baggage. She felt she had been attacked by "Black People" at the brokerage house, and this ultimately led to the loss of her job and hospitalization. In an effort to prove her point, she had created, what was, to her, irrefutable evidence that her attack and abduction were absolutely true. Her proof? She had created a series of watercolor drawings showing how little black people had indeed actually come into her brokerage office and spirited her away. It was all I could do to mollify her and explain that the time was not right to take action against her abductors. I kept this delaying tactic going for fifteen years until she passed away.

My client came to see me many times after I became her trustee. I meted out money to her on a weekly basis from the trust fund her father had lovingly created for her.

For several years when I first became a lawyer, I, like many other neophyte lawyers did almost anything to try and drum up business. I had learned that there was a support group of new attorneys that met, exchanged ideas, and horror stories of life in the trenches. At the beginning of the last meeting that I attended, the president of the organization opened the meeting with a small speech. He stated that his practice had experienced an unexpected surge of popularity, and he felt it was time to step down as president. "In fact", he continued, "my practice has become so self sufficient, that I am now going to limit myself to the representation of sane people".

Obviously, my practice had not reached such a lofty pinnacle. In fact, after thirty years of practice, it still hasn't.

One day after a visit from my client for her weekly stipend, my secretary approached me. She asked me if I was aware that my client had appropriated some of my stationary. I thanked her and assured her I had not given my client permission to use my letterhead.

At our next meeting, I asked my client if she had taken my letterhead without my permission. She seemed non-plused by the act and was quite upbeat about it. She explained to me that while she was a stockbroker, she had one client who she did an enormous amount of research. She stated that her research had earned many millions of dollars for this particular client. She was owed compensation for her work!

On my letterhead, she had submitted a bill to her former client for six million dollars. Not to worry, she assured me that I would be on for my one-third share as her attorney.

Damned if I did not closely check my mail for the next several weeks.

Why We Hate Lawyers I

Background:

Throughout the history of the law, there are rules concerning whether contracts (or agreements) have to be put in writing. American law, for the most part, insists that agreements be reduced to writing, but verbal contracts are allowed to be honored, under certain circumstances (though it is rumored that Samuel Goldwyn, old time movie mogul, stated a verbal contract is not worth the paper it is written on).

The Statute of Frauds is an old time concept of law that states that all dealings with real property (i.e. land and buildings) be in writing. It obviously evolved from the point of view that dealing with real property was so important (and for the most part, one of the larger transactions that a person would be involved with in their life) that to avoid ambiguity of verbal statements, deals were only enforceable if they were reduced to writing.

Two sophisticated lawyers were in the midst of a complicated lawsuit whose subject matter was establishing the amount of money one party would be paying the other party for the transferal of a piece of property that was the subject matter of a long and complicated WRITTEN contract between their respective clients.

During the formation of a lawsuit, and even as the lawsuit commences, a judge will try to force combatants to settling the case.

A judge does this for practical considerations. First, one never knows, in an adversarial situation, what the finding will be, by a jury, or even a judge. Remember, in any case, unless there actually is a settlement between the parties, one party is earmarked to be a winner while the other party will be bitterly disappointed. (I can assure you that unless a lawyer is saddled with an absolute loser, both participants in a lawsuit feel that they have a "good shot" to win their case).

The second reason a judge will intervene in the lawsuit, is for the obvious reason of saving the court's time. A settlement in a lawsuit that is scheduled for a week's worth of trial time can be a tremendous drain on the court docket, not to mention the judge's time. Eliminating a weeks worth of trial time will be an enormous boost to the court.

Back to the case. During this particular lawsuit, the judge continually tried valiantly to force the combatant lawyers to try and come up with a monetary figure that would end the case. There would be testimony in court and the trial would plod along.

At each break, the judge would call the attorneys for an informal bashing of the attorneys for their continued truculence.

Finally, even the attorneys became tired of the controversy, and they stood before the judge during a break when the jury had been brought back to the jury room. Both attorneys stated that they had agreed on a dollar amount for the transference of the property from one party to the other. The judge asked, and the attorney's responded that their respective clients also agreed upon the settlement figure. They recited the settlement figure to the judge in open court.

I also point out that during all court cases, all of the verbal utterances in court are taken down either by a stenographer, or at least a tape recording is made.

When the judge heard the good news, he was ecstatic. He profusely thanked the participating lawyers, stated a timetable for the transference of the property and passing of the sale price, and dismissed the parties with the blessing of the court.

All would seem well except for the unthinkable. One of the parties of the suit decided that they didn't like the settlement after all, didn't think it was fair, and wanted to resume the trial.

Of course, resuming the trial was out of the question, as the jury had been dismissed, and essentially the case had been concluded. Perhaps a more prudent attorney would have or should have counseled his client that the case was actually done, and the parties were bound by the agreement that had been reached. Counsel should have impressed upon his client that what had taken place between the parties, and among the parties and the court was as strong and ironclad as any written document that would have been crafted by either attorney.

Upon the pressing by the client, his attorney stated that there was one obscure chance to throw a monkey wrench into the court settled agreement, and that would be to invoke the Statute of Frauds. After all, the attorneys had not reached the decision by a "writing", it had been agreed upon verbally in open court and therefore "had not been reduced to writing". (Although, at some point it certainly would have been reduced to writing). For instance, when the stenographer would transcribe the court case, if necessary, then the statements made in court would have been reduced to writing. But the fact remained, the lawyer concluded, the original settlement had been verbal, and not in writing. Therefore, the selling price "had not been reduced to writing, and therefore should not be honored". The client's attorney should have had the integrity to stand up against his client's desperate grasping at straws, but of course, since his client also paid the bills, his attorney was accommodating his client's desperation.

The objecting lawyer petitioned the court to set aside the "verbal" agreement, and order a new trial. The judge, to his credit, rejected the petitioning lawyer's position and upheld the settlement hammered out in front of him.

He pointed out that the necessity to have the agreement reduced to writing was not necessary given the arena it was stated in and with the parties in attendance that the statement was made - the judge and his court.

The objecting lawyer was not done! He actually appealed the decision to the appeals court. Aside from the eighteen months tied up in appeals, and the accompanying cost of doing the appeal, to their credit the Appeals Court upheld the lower court's decision.

The Witness

Background:

The judge, aside from being a skilled jurist, fully knowledgeable in the laws and how these laws should be applied to the problem at hand, is also a person excelling in the sociology connected with legal situations and dealing with people of a very diverse background.

The judge has to skillfully make rulings concerning the trial at hand. And while the judge is making the judicial decisions to keep the trial moving along smoothly, he or she attempts to make decisions or explanations to mollify the parties who become disgruntled at not receiving the ruling that they are seeking.

When I was doing public defending, I was assigned a homeowner who did not have the usual credentials of a lifelong petty (or worse) criminal.

This gentleman had no record at all. His sin was that he was accused of trespassing on his neighbor's property. It seems that he and his neighbor had been at each other's throats for over twenty years for a grievance that had been long forgotten.

However, the animosity remained strong, and the bad blood, at least on my client's accuser's side, knew no bounds.

The accuser had brought his complaint to the district court. The way you initiate a criminal case is you make an accusation against somebody, and either a magistrate of the court, or a judge himself, listens to the accuser make his accusation against the purported wrongdoer. At this stage, the magistrate or judge does not rule whether the purported defendant is guilty of the complained of offense, just whether that what the accuser is saying, rises to the level of a criminal act as stated. (For instance, a person coming into court claiming that a party swore at him would not establish a criminal complaint because, if the party did swear at the victim, that act in and of itself would not constitute a criminal act.)

My client was not so lucky. It was a simple enough allegation against him. He had supposedly gone on the property that was not his. Unlike more complex situations, this fact pattern was fairly cut and dried. It was just labeled trespassing.

I was assigned the case at arraignment, where the accused is read exactly what his crime is (the arraignment). The next step is a pretrial. At a pretrial, where the government might be inclined to settle or compromise the case, neither side was interested. The accuser wanted blood and my client was not going to admit to a charge that he vehemently denied. We received our trial date.

We show up on the day of trial. As we prepare for trial, the court calls us up for a side bar. (Side bars are when the court calls the two attorneys up to talk to the judge, usually out of earshot of the jury, or even "one on one" with the judge (with both lawyers) where one of the attorneys feels the issue to be addressed would be better suited as a mini debate, rather than the formality of open court.)

When we go up for this side bar, not only I and the Assistant District Attorney go to the side bar, but the Assistant District Attorney also brings up the party bringing the complaint, the accuser.

Me: "Your Honor this is highly improper...."
Judge: "Mr. Weiss, shut up"

Me:	"Yes Judge"
ADA:	"Your Honor, my client has an unusual request that I can't seem to dissuade him of, "May he ask you?"
Judge:	"Yes, sure"
Accuser:	"Your Honor, I would like my dog to testify."
Me:	"The dog is not on the witness list"
Judge:	"Mr. Weiss, one more word…"
Me:	"Yes, your Honor"
Judge:	"Mr. Accuser, what do you mean, you want your dog to testify?"
Accuser:	"Your honor when the defendant came upon my property, my dog went crazy. He hates the defendant and always barks incessantly when the defendant walks in front of my house."
Judge:	"and…"
Accuser:	"My dog went crazy the day the defendant trespassed upon my property. He can verify that the defendant trespassed on my property."
Judge:	"But Mr. Accuser, can't you see the problems that allowing the dog to testify."
Accuser:	"No, he will prove that the Defendant trespassed on the property"
Judge:	"No, sir, I can't allow your dog to testify. For instance, how are we going to swear him in. If we can't swear him in, he is not under oath to tell the truth. How will I know if he is lying?"
Accuser:	"But…"
Judge:	"Also the defendant's attorney has a right to cross examine each witness. How is he going to be able to cross examine your dog?"
Accuser:	"But your Honor, he knows the defendant trespassed…"

Attorney Richard Weiss

Judge: "Sorry, I've made my ruling, please step back".

The judge had strong resolve and did not change her mind. The accuser was beside himself. The judge ruled that there was not enough evidence to find my client guilty of trespassing.

You would think that that would be the end of it, but the accuser actually appealed the judge's ruling.

Needless to say, the judge and her ruling were upheld.

The Oldest Profession

Background:

The structure of the court system is the ADA's, Assistant District Attorneys, are the first wave of legal representatives, representing the interest of the state for which they work. In the legal setting, which is the district court in most states (one step down from the superior court or supreme court, which hears the most serious cases), cases come to be heard where the participants are the Assistant District Attorney, representing the interests of the state, and a private attorney (or a public defender if the defendant cannot afford an attorney) representing the interests of the accused.

For lower level crimes, i.e. shoplifting, simple assault, driving under the influence of alcohol, disorderly conduct, the system works by most cases being resolved by "a deal". If it is the perpetrator's first offense, he might seek to obtain a CWOF (which is explained elsewhere in this book). Deals originate with the Assistant District Attorney being locked into some arrangement, but anything ultimately agreed upon will have the imprimatur of the judge.

On the other hand, the judge, at least in theory, attempts to honor the "deals" made by his or her Assistant District Attorneys. But though a judge will pay lip service to this concept, the judge, if he or she has a strong opinion or conviction about the case, will make sure the agreement reflects exactly what the judge wants it to say.

Just recently, a former employee of mine began making her money in the trenches, "public defending". This consists of going to the District Courts and being assigned various cases of people who are indigent.

On one of her duty days, she gets assigned a "pre-op" transsexual (going from male to female).

The defendant is a sweet thing, not wanting to go toe to toe with the more hard core cases (male) that he/she might encounter in jail. You can well imagine that things would not go too easily for him/her if he/she was put in jail.

In fact, when my ex-employee got her case, the client had already been arrested several times for prostitution and had developed a singular loathing and aversion to being put back in jail. This aversion to jail did not curtail her still attempting to ply her trade, perhaps in a limited fashion on the mean streets of Boston.

Her latest peccadillo did not have to do with hooking, as it were, but with lewd and lascivious behavior. She had been apprehended for flashing her breasts in public, I am sure with an eye towards more illegal endeavors, but nevertheless, for the time being, her transgression was only indecent behavior.

The defendant implored my ex-employee to do whatever it took to keep him/her out of jail. However, the facts of the case seemed to make it an open and shut affair. Certainly the several officers who had apprehended her, and the ensuing write-up, were quite in order. It seemed like a slam dunk, as they say.

Then, my ex-employee had a brainstorm. She picked up on the fact that our pre-op transsexual was still a man. And if we were going to get into a pissing contest of whether he was still a man after his hardware was going to be removed, we did not have to cross that bridge because he had not had that part of the treatment, the significant operation.

He had had the treatment to enhance his breasts, and my ex-employee informed me that they were quite spectacular, given the circumstances.

My ex-employee went to work to see what law there was, and whether in fact he could be charged with lewd and lascivious behavior, given the fact that he was still an unequivocal man.

Much to her delight there was sparse previous case law on this point, and nothing to implicate this "man' s" actions as being anything against the law. After all, a "man" could flash his breasts in public. Perhaps the court system could attempt to charge him with disorderly conduct, but certainly with no overtones of lewd and lascivious behavior, which was the far more serious offense.

The closest case law came to this situation was when a fairly obese man was cited for lewdness for just wearing a thong on a beach. However, this case was not really on point and the finding was for the obese man anyway.

The court schedules a pre-trial conference and the Assistant District Attorney tries to hammer out what he felt was a fair compromise, a finding of guilty and thirty days in jail.

When my ex-employee rejects any type of guilt or jail time, everyone can see the case is heading for the judge's tutelage.

The case is called in court and the ADA and my ex-employee stand up and start squabbling with each other. My ex-employee has the presence of mind to suggest a side bar, and both attorneys trudge up to the judge. The judge surprisingly is concerned with the case and turns to my ex-employee and addresses her. He asks what the problem is, the facts are open and shut, and the Assistant District Attorney seems to be offering a fair sentence.

My ex-employee then drops her bombshell. She states to the judge that in her opinion, she does not think the state has any case at all, and the whole complaint should be dismissed.

The judge incredulously asks what the basis of her statement is, and she is more than happy to respond! He's a man He did not violate any law in flashing his breasts.

The Assistant District Attorney is chatting away like a gnat, which is irritating everybody. The judge, far more sophisticated, sees the beauty in my ex-employee's position. His face turns a strange color of pale white and his eyes begin to role in his head. He addresses the Assistant District Attorney, "What law do we have on this?" The ADA responds that this is the first he's heard of this defense.

"Go do some research and come back for a second call", the judge bellows.

One hour later, everybody is back in court and the case is called to the bench.

JUDGE: "Did you have any luck finding some law on this?"

ADA: "No, your honor."

JUDGE: "How are we going to proceed?"

ADA: "Your honor, I am sure I can persuade a jury that his actions were lewd and lascivious."

JUDGE: "You just don't get it. You may be able to persuade a jury, but that might not be the law. The law has to match up to the act!"

ADA: "But, your honor...

JUDGE "I DON'T CARE IF YOU THINK YOU (with a flourish to ADA) CAN WIN. I'M NOT GOING TO BE THE JUDGE THAT IS KNOWN AS THE BOOB JUDGE OR THE JUDGE THAT OPENED THE FLOODGATES FOR TRANSSEXUALS PRANCING AROUND WITH

THEIR TITS HANGING OUT. DO I MAKE MYSELF CLEAR?"

ADA: "But, Judge..."

JUDGE: "DO I MAKE MYSELF CLEAR?"

ADA: "Yes Judge."

Turning to my ex-employee, the judge asks if it will be all right if the Commonwealth (of Massachusetts) dismisses her client's case. "Of course, your honor", responds my cx- employee.

There was one happy transsexual that night.

In the Parking Lot

Perhaps craziness runs in a family. Actually, geneticists believe this to be true.

The nephew of the gentleman who wanted to blow away his cheating wife was my primary client. I had represented him in a bankruptcy and we easily slipped into the divorce between himself and his wife.

As some divorces go, this one was filled with vitriol. Much of the animosity and ill will could be ascribed to my client.

My client was a little crazy and he made me a little uneasy. After several skirmishes in court, I told my client that I felt we should part ways. I did not like the position he took or the courses of action that he either tacitly or overtly suggested I do. He shared with me some of his thoughts. They were dangerous in the extreme. Perhaps he had learned his critical thinking at the knee of his uncle. He was unfazed. I believe he was looking forward to representing himself. I find many of my clients (as well as just plain acquaintances) have a secret desire to take a crack at lawyering. They dream that if they just had the opportunity to cross examine that person that they find annoying or distasteful, they would certainly be able to reduce their adversary to a sniveling groveling mess. . . .

My client had been accused of spreading a deadly chemical fertilizer, Chlordane, around the outside of the family home. He was now persona non-gratis at the home, could not visit with his children, and made the wife fearful of him.

Since this chemical was toxic, the allegation was serious and the court and judge wanted to become involved. There were minor children involved who liked to play outside the house.

Since I was handling his other case, I was seeing him on a weekly basis and he kept me informed of the wrangling of the divorce. He related to me that he had been informed by the court that there would be a hearing on this matter.

On the appointed day, he drives to the court and parks in the parking lot. As luck would have it, his wife and her attorney appear in the parking lot at almost the same time.

His wife yells out "Why are you jeopardizing the safety of your children." Our hero responds that he doesn't know what she is talking about.

The lawyer mixes in "We have a picture of you doing it"

"Impossible, it's not me"

"The picture doesn't lie"

"May I see the picture"?

Where upon the lawyer opens his briefcase and rummages around. Straightens up, proud as a peacock, puffs out his chest and hands him a picture of our hero certainly looking like he is spreading something on the perimeter of the house.

"I ate the picture", my ex-client informs me.

Closing Argument

A fairly accomplished criminal attorney had been saddled by the state with representing a man charged with murder.

The state's case was overwhelming in all aspects except they did not have a body. This usually is the foundation of any murder prosecution. But in this case, the State had to make do with what they had, or rather, did not have.

This fact had given the defense attorney a glimmer of hope. Testimony at trial, in spite of no corpse, had not gone well. Circumstantial evidence was overwhelming. Testimony against his client had been devastating. Nevertheless, the attorney had crafted a plan.

The trial was over and it was time for final arguments The defense attorney, the first to speak, began:

"Ladies and gentlemen of the jury. You have heard the prosecution's case. They are trying to convince you that the State has proven their case, and that my client has murdered Mr. Jones. But they have not produced Mr. Jones' body. In fact, ladies and gentlemen, they cannot produce Mr. Jones' body, because Mr. Jones is not dead! I have asked Mr. Jones to come to court to show you he is not dead, and he will walk through those doors in the next three to five minutes."

A hush falls over the court and you can hear a pin drop. The jury's attention is fixated on the courtroom door.

Attorney Richard Weiss

One minute, two minutes, three minutes, nothing. Four and then five minutes... Finally, the judge steps in "Mr. Attorney. . ."

The defense attorney whirls towards the jury and says: "Ladies and Gentlemen, Mr. Jones will not be walking through the door because frankly, I do not know where he is. But what I did do was build your anticipation, and frankly, I bet every one of you had expected Mr. Jones to come walking through that door. What I did do was create reasonable doubt. If I can create reasonable doubt as to whether Mr. Jones is dead, and if you have reasonable doubt, you must acquit my client, that is the law. Thank you."

And with that, the attorney sits down.

The jury leaves to deliberate, and our attorney's chest is almost bursting with encouragement. This was his finest closing, and he could see that the jury bought it. He pulled out victory from the jaws of defeat.

The jury comes back, and much to the dismay of the attorney, they find the client guilty of first-degree murder. The attorney is devastated. He can't understand how he lost the case.

He packed up his briefcase, assures his poor client he has a chance on appeal and starts going back to his office.

As he leaves the courthouse, he happens to bump into one of the female jurors.

"May I speak with you," he politely asks. She nods her assent.

"How could you find my client guilty? Each and every one of you had your eyes riveted to the courtroom door. I created reasonable doubt."

Juror: "It is true that everyone in the courtroom was transfixed on the courtroom door, except for one person, and that was your client. He was looking straight ahead – he knew Mr. Jones would not be walking into the courtroom."

A Lifetime Job

Background:

When one comes to the legal system to embark on a case, a person is looking for truth and justice.

A court of law will render a decision on a dispute in one of two basic ways.

The first and most popular function of a court trial is that the court will try and determine who is right where the facts involved between the parties are hotly disputed. For instance, two combatants come into court; each convinced that the other party ran a red light. This is a dispute obvious upon the "facts." It is up to the trier of fact, either a jury, or a judge designated to determine the facts, that indeed will determine who ran that red light. This is the more common situation of a lawsuit.

The second type of case is where the facts are not in dispute, but the interpretation of the law is in question.

An example of this second situation would be where two sides to a controversy both agree that a party had been driving his vehicle at sixty miles per hour. They also agree that the driver was apprehended by the police equidistant between a sign that you could go sixty miles per hour and a sign that said you could go only fifty miles per hour. In this example, since all facts are agreed upon between the parties, the issue becomes what the legal driving limit would be in a fact pattern such as this. The answer would be found by the application of existing laws. This function becomes the obligation of the court and judges to interpret the laws, not a jury to decide who did what, as stated above, because the facts themselves were not in dispute.

Therefore when the facts are not in dispute, it falls upon the shoulders of a judge to interpret the law.

There are many stories of a person being caught up by circumstance beyond his or her control that can dictate what their life is today, or unfortunately what their life is going to be in the long run. The long run can be weeks, but it could be years. In fact, this is the foundation of what good novels are made of.

Unfortunately, if the person is desperate enough or so caught up in their own personal soap opera, they can create their own hell in any situation, and unfortunately the law can occasionally accommodate that hell that they have created.

A female client comes to my office She is educated with a PhD, and she had been married to a doctor. They had two girls together.

Twenty years ago, when the children were young, they went ahead with a divorce. Unfortunately, at that time, all issues of the divorce had not been addressed.

Since they were young and beginning their careers, there was no property to speak of to be divided up, so the divorce essentially focused on the important matters, child custody, visitation, and child support. The divorce was contested (meaning the two parties could not agree upon matters without the intervention of the court). We now have divorces, either contested or uncontested where not only are all issues addressed, but they are addressed by the court insisting that both parties submit an elaborate and extensive written agreement that attempts to address ALL matters between the parties. Presumably with this document there will be no issue left unaddressed.

This action was contested, and the parties themselves were on a budgetary shoestring, so some issues were left out. Now, twenty years later, the ex wife wanted her pound of flesh.

The two main issues that had not been addressed twenty years ago were alimony and the division of a pension plan that the doctor had. Usually, the statute of limitations would somehow kick in and limit one's rights after such a long time. In a case where the statute of limitations does come into play, twenty years would easily exceed any statue of limitations. But here, several factors allowed these two issues to remain on the table. First, because we were in probate (Family) court, the court retains wide jurisdiction over matters that are brought to it and litigated in court. Next, because the pension issue had not been addressed, it would have been unfair not to address it at all. Finally, the alimony issue did not exist while the children were minors (i.e., to some extent, child support embraces "some" alimony considerations when child support is being paid). Now, child support had been extinguished, so alimony was an open question, so long as the ex wife had not remarried.

The wife now comes and hires a lawyer to address the above two issues. The lawyer charged her "by the hour" and her money long ran out before she could bring this matter to trial.

She found her way to me and I agreed to take my fee AFTER we had won, always a dicey proposition.

When I evaluated the case, it seemed to me that she had devoted her life in one way or another to attacking her successful husband. My client was attractive and shrewd, and I hypothesized she had not remarried for the sole reason to keep her alimony claims alive, and consequently keep her contact with her ex husband, no matter how attenuated it was.

Settlement talks with the other side were fruitless. This was so because my client was dead set on having her "day in court" and nothing short of the doctor turning over his whole net worth to her was going to dissuade my client from her trial.

The scheduled trial day came. I had prepared my client for trial and she was chomping at the bit, so to speak, for her to have her say in court.

The daughters were more or less on her side and the mother and two daughters were set to testify.

We started the trial. The judge asked each counsel if he were prepared to give a summary of each parties' case. This is quite common as it is usually called an opening statement that the attorney addresses the judge (or jury). This opening statement is usually a summary of what their whole case is about. However, the statement is only supposed to be a summary, and not an in depth discourse. It is also not to be considered as evidence that a judge or jury can rely upon. The opening statement is meant solely to be a preview of what evidence will be presented at trial from the point of view of each respective attorney.

However, here, the judge made it clear that he was going to want each attorney to summarize each client's position in its entirety. (I believe the judge felt that the facts that were going to be testified to were not really in dispute. Therefore, by laying out our respective clients' positions, we were really getting to say what was going to be testified to at trial with minimum harassment from the other side.) The judge concluded that this would be the most expedient way for him to learn about the case.

Facts such as how much the doctor was making, or how much an ex spouse was entitled to for alimony were more a "matter of law" then a question of fact. In other words, the facts were not in dispute (i.e. the doctor was known to make an amount of money and not contested by us). Therefore, it would be the judge's obligation to say where a party makes "X"; then, alimony should by "Y".

I had never participated in a trial in quite this manner, but I followed the judge's directives.

I had a fairly detailed summary of my client's legal objectives, factual statements as to how much she was making versus her husband's rather generous salary, value of the doctor's pension fund, then and now. I relayed my total spiel in my "opening" statement and was satisfied that my client's total case was laid out for the judge in an accurate and comprehensive manner.

Opposing counsel then relayed his client's case in similar fashion. The judge had been correct in that facts and statements being made by both attorneys were not too dissimilar in content, nor were they so inflammatory that either side had any serious objections to the content of what the other side stated. When facts are not in dispute, it is the court and not a jury (or a trier of facts) that determines the outcome.

After both attorneys had given their synopses, the judge asked my client if there were anything that she would like to add.

Taken aback at first, my client rallied and took this unexpected opportunity to take the stand to testify. However, she found herself with little to say as I had done a pretty good job of covering all the bases. She testified to a few things, repeated several facts that I had already laid out, and in general, was a bit cranky as to everything that was going on.

When the judge asked if she had anything else to say, she sheepishly replied no.

The doctor had nothing more to add.

The judge concluded matters by announcing that he felt that he had heard enough for him to render a correct judgment in this matter.

He then dismissed us.

Attorney Richard Weiss

All hell broke loose in the corridor outside the courtroom. My client, with her daughters feebly backing her up, clamored that she wanted her day in court and she had been denied it.

I could not console her, but I also did not agree with her. She went storming off.

My client was in constant touch with me after that continually complaining. I told her that nothing much could be done until the judge made a ruling.

Several months later a judgment did come down. The judge awarded us part of the doctor's pension, less than what we thought fair, alimony, less than what we thought was fair, and a retroactive date for calculation of payment, going back less than we thought it should. Nevertheless we got something, and that should have brought this long odyssey to a close.

Not for my client. She wanted to appeal. Not so much for the judge's decisions, but for the way the judge conducted the trial. For her, at least, I think what the judge did was a godsend for her. As I have said, I think she wanted to make this her life's work. If she could not have him, then she could endlessly harass him. She could be intertwined by the slender thread of him being obligated to pay weekly alimony, but from her point of view, she still wanted more, anything to keep the contact alive!

My client found an attorney to appeal the case. After several years of waiting, the appeals court upheld the judge's actions.

I, of course, parted ways with her after the trial. However, five years after the trial, I still see her frequenting the probate court. I do not even want to know what concept she has conjured up to keep this matter there, still alive.

Work Study

Background:

In some regards, the legal system is very caring and sympathetic. As harsh as they might be in some situations (the three strike rule where if you are convicted of two felonies, and you have the misfortune of a third encounter with the law, no matter if this third offense is truly minor, you might end up doing ten years because you are "a three time loser"). Also, some mandatory sentencing, like losing your license to drive for certain driving infractions, sometimes can seem harsh.

However, on the other hand, the law is often forgiving. CWOF'S, continued without a finding is a very fair and widely applied concept. The court, for a wide range of infractions, some serious (assault, robbery) and some not so serious, shoplifting or some traffic infractions, will accept your admission of guilt, put you on a type of mini probation for a period of anywhere from three months to two years, and if you do not get into further trouble, will wipe the case off of your record if you have behaved for that stated period.

In this vein, in some jurisdictions the court has even gone one step further. Depending on the problem, the court system and probation offices will truly go lightly on a child or young adult, a first timer, who has been unlucky enough to have his first brush with the law.

For the court system to do this, the complained of offense must also be of the minor type.

I had a friend who was a teacher for an inner city junior high. She informed me that one of her charges had a run in with the law, and seeing that the young man was poor, she wanted to show this boy that the world was not out to get him. She thought my personal representation would show this boy that there were people out there who cared.

The sentence the court was willing to assign consisted of the youngster doing public services hours. Doing public service is a common punishment to assign to a non- dangerous criminal who the court system is not out to crucify. The punishment will obviously be menial and low grade, sweeping streets, cleaning beaches etc. In this case, the offender was even luckier, in that the program offered to the party was even more benign. The youth would never have to even see a judge, so if the scenario ever was created where the young offender was put in a position of being asked "did you ever go before a judge" the youthful offender could honestly answer that he had not.

The day came to initiate the process. My friend took the student himself to the court where he was to meet me. It seems he had run afoul at his job, enough to find himself in this predicament. My friend had not told me what his problem had been.

I met this fellow early in the morning at court, and he was even grumbling about the time of day. The first thing out of his mouth was that he didn't understand why he was even there at court.

I asked him what he had done. He responded that he was in a work-study program and he went to a prominent restaurant almost every day. He said he checked in with my friend (his teacher) and he was working at the restaurant to get school credit.

"What do you do?" I asked

"I pick up tips" he responded

"What do you mean, pick up tips" I clearly asked.

"You know, when a customer finishes his meal, he usually leaves a tip. I pick them up."

"And then you give the tip to the waitresses?"

"No, I keep them."

I was taken aback. "Don't you think you should give them to the waitresses, that is what they earned for waiting on the customers?"

His response, "Naw, that's my job."

The court allowed him to go through this special program to protect his reputation, but he was still grumbling. He could still not understand what he had done wrong.

I am not sure this boy was going to be a candidate for the clean record club, but he could never say he wasn't given a fair chance.

Good work if you can find it.

The Rules

Background:

Motion session. When a lawsuit is brought, the court system takes over jurisdiction and the case revolves around the court. As the lawsuit progresses, minor situations arise that have to be addressed. Either new information needs to be integrated, or requests to depose (question) the other side, orders limiting certain information, or in other situations, orders allowing a bevy of things that needs to be adjusted or tweaked, is accomplished through motions.

In this particular episode, the motion session was for family law. Things such as child support, disputes over paternity, arrearage of child support payments, visitation of parents, were addressed.

While lawyers obviously learn a rather significant amount of things (i.e. laws, procedure, and negotiating techniques) we rely upon a relatively brief set of rules numbered 1-70 called Massachusetts Rules of Civil Procedure (MRCP). These rules are fairly standard through out the country and are even similar to the corresponding Federal Rules of Civil Procedure (how cases are conducted in Federal court).

Each corresponding rule has a number, and because rules addressing certain situations are more important than others (i.e. I think that almost everyone knows the number 401K is for retirement issues), we as lawyers get to be comfortable in referring to certain actions that

Attorney Richard Weiss

we take by the corresponding rule number. A rule 12-B-6 motion is accusing the other side of not knowing what they are talking about and an attempt to stop the lawsuit because a lawyer has "Failed to State a claim for which relief can be granted." A rule 41 dismissal suggests both parties are agreeing to end the lawsuit. Rule 4 attacks the sufficiency of whether the other side has been properly served the paperwork of the lawsuit itself.

On this particular day, my client and I were in court to get increased child support from my client's husband. Child support is based on the salaries of both parents. The relevant law that we were going under was rule 410 of the probate rules. The judge on duty that day had a reputation of being eccentric, so you really never knew what to expect.

I was third or fourth to be called in the motion session before the above judge that I was to plead my case. I had not been paying close attention to the three who went before me, so I was unprepared for what happened.

When we were called before the judge, instead of addressing the issue and having the expected skirmish between husband and wife, the judge asked if I had notified the Department of Revenue of this hearing. Since neither parent was indigent, or had any dealing with the Department of Revenue, this notice was not necessary.

The judge would not listen to the facts of the case between husband and wife. I was dispatched to give notice to the Department of Revenue and inform the court when I accomplished this.

As I waited in court, every lawyer that was called up to the judge met the same fate. As you can imagine, each attorney had a different issue to discuss with the judge, but it did not matter to this judge on this particular day.

It was as if the judge had nothing to do the previous night and had refreshed himself with the rules, dwelling on obscure and inappropriate rules and procedure, and throwing a monkey wrench into the whole motion session.

Time and time again, a lawyer would advance his case, and each time the judge would respond with some numbered rule that the lawyer was not familiar with. A lawyer would state "I am seeking visitation for my client on every other Saturday", and the judge would interrupt with ""Did you comply with rule 18?" The lawyer would be forced to admit that he was unfamiliar with rule 18, and the judge would unceremoniously dispatch him to "check it out" and come back when he complied.

This happened to each and every lawyer scheduled to be heard that morning. Absolutely nobody escaped. And these lawyers were not rookies. While some might have been lightly experienced, others had twenty to thirty years under their belt. The judges actions were both silly and infantile, but more importantly, incorrect!

Not only did this disrupt the lawyers' schedules, but it also wreaked havoc on the court session.

Because no lawyer made it unscathed through the morning, everybody and every case had to be addressed in the afternoon. The only problem was that there was a whole new contingent of cases scheduled for the afternoon. The judge was now saddled with the unenviable task of addressing a double session for the afternoon. The session turned into a circus. Cases were called up and the judge just gave lip service to the facts. Carefully reasoned decisions and the expectation of the Wisdom of Solomon was out the window. The judge was mired in the quicksand of his own doing. Who knows what he felt he accomplished or even whether the judge felt his actions were abnormal.

I heard for weeks after this fiasco that attorneys had to go into court again, usually in front of the same judge, to remedy the silly results that that judge rendered during that session.

Clothes Make the Man

A divorce attorney gets a call from a new client. This attractive, middle-aged lady was hell bent on obtaining a divorce.

The attorney meets with the woman. As one can imagine, there are many reasons why people divorce, not all of them logical or sensible. This case was particularly vexing.

The client paints a picture of a loving relationship. Her husband is actually not a Neanderthal, but a caring "metrosexual" who was considerate of her every whim.

He was good to their children. He remembered birthdays and anniversaries. He didn't watch football on Sundays, and actually looked forward to family vacations.

What in the world, then, was the reason for the divorce.

"He cheated on me" was her succinct reply. All the rest came into perspective. The ultimate betrayal for some, and they will not allow the deed to be rectified, mollified, or dissipated.

The lawyer had heard enough. From that point, the lawyer and client go full tilt.

They serve discovery on the lawyer the husband had been forced to employ.

Even as they interacted, the wife's lawyer also found the husband charming.

At this point the wife's lawyer realized she had not asked the sixty-four dollar question of her client, exactly how did you catch your husband cheating on you?

"A package from Victoria's Secret came to the house. It had underwear, a chemise, a garter belt… "

I get the picture", her lawyer said

The case moved forward and finally it was time to depose the husband.

When a person is deposed, the participants usually are the person being deposed, his attorney, the lawyer for the party he or she is representing, and the stenographer. The legal rules usually allow the other party to attend the deposition – if he or she remains quiet. Usually you have a situation where the observing party chomps at the bit to interject his or her two cents worth, but, by the rules they have to remain silent.

The attorney begins the questioning, and it is all the wife can do to restrain herself as the husband attempts to answer the lawyer's questions.

Finally the lawyer rolls around to the adultery.

"Are you seeing any other woman?"

Husband: "of course not"
Attorney: "Have you had lunch with any female in the last six months?"
Husband: "of course not"
Attorney: "Have you had sex with any one else except your wife in the last six months?"
Husband: "absolutely not"

At this point, contrary to the lawyers strict admonition of not saying anything during the questioning, the wife goes ballistic. She starts swearing at her husband, calling him a filthy liar, and not understanding how he could be allowed to walk this earth.

In response to this tirade, the husband reiterates his position that he doesn't even understand what he did wrong. The wife responds with a continuing tirade. "You punk, you are lavishing lingerie, underwear, things you never bought me on your little floozie.

Husband: You're crazy, I don't know what your talking about. There's no one but you.

Wife, with a flourish, whips out a package that she has with her. Panties, bras, garter belts tumble onto the table.

"What the fuck is this", the wife screams, as a hunter lording over her kill.

The husband's eyes bulge a little. He handles the items with a loving hand that only the owner of such items would exhibit.

He regains his composure and somewhat startling says "Did you bother to check out the size of these things!"

Everybody in the deposition fights for a gulp of air. The husband continues. "For Christ's sakes, these items are mine, they were sent to me! I was wondering what happened to that order."

No Good Turn Goes Unpunished

Background:

The Board of Bar overseers is the policing unit for attorneys. Lawyers have a code of ethics that they must follow. Some rules, such as avoiding conflict of interests are well known to the lay public. Other rules, such as the prohibition of lending money to one's clients are less well known.

A client comes to me with damage to her wrist in an automobile accident. Most of my practice consists of smallish type automobile accidents. This client fit into this category. Initially, it looked as if she would treat with either a chiropractor or physical therapist for several months. She would heal sufficiently and the case would be worth five to ten thousand dollars.

Damages for a case are usually based on two measurements. First, if there is any permanent damage, such as scarring or diminished use of my client's wrist, then this constitutes a damage that compensation is based on. In fact, permanent damage usually suggests more monetary awards then the five or ten thousand dollars that I suggested above.

If damage is not permanent, a person might suffer lingering damage that stretches out over weeks and months. This is called temporary damage.

The number of weeks or months that a person is saddled by these "temporary" damages is the measure that is used to establish an amount of money for compensation. A person is entitled to be compensated for the time he is convalescing from his injury. This type of damage is manifested by a nagging pain that afflicts the person even though the person might be able to work. A more serious injury might manifest itself by the victim losing several weeks of work. However, the injury itself is characterized by the fact that it is temporary in nature, and the victim usually completely heals by the end of his or her disability period. (The disability period is defined by the time a victim is suffering the effects of the accident). This damage is usually called temporary disability, and is mostly the basis for my five to ten thousand dollar cases.

My client's case seemed initially to fall in this latter category. The first report from the doctor suggested there was no permanent injury and she should heal in due course. Due course in this case would be several months.

Well, something funny happened on the way to the settlement table. Instead of the wrist healing up, it became worse. Instead of a projected two to four months to heal, my client was in no better shape six months after the accident.

This fact had two startling consequences. First, the insurance company had begun increasingly to become aggressive to settle the case.

An insurance company, upon the receipt of notice of an injury, establishes a "reserve", an amount of money that they estimate will take to settle the case. This allows the insurance company to set its insurance rates for the following year. Rates are based on how many and for how much a company's total claims were for the previous year. A claims adjustor, the person from the insurance company who handles the claim, also has an interest in addressing his cases and keeping things moving along.

I received up-to-date medical reports apprising me that the wrist injury was far more serious than originally thought. Therefore, I was being pressured by the insurance company to take the five thousand dollars offered, and I had to counter with the fact that first, my client had not reached an "end result", a time when we felt comfortable that we could completely quantify the extent of the injury, and more importantly, the case was going to be far more valuable then the five thousand dollars that they were offering me.

Things began to become quite acrimonious between myself and the insurance adjuster. I believe the insurance companies see so many quasi-legitimate claims, that the insurance company had a hard time adjusting their thinking that this injury had matured to a legitimate claim that not only broke the mold of a minor accident, but was looming to cost the company significantly more money.

The second consequence of all of this was that my client was becoming desperate for a settlement. The longer the case went on, the more financially strapped my client became.

As I said in the opening Background, one of the caveats of being an attorney is not to lend money to clients. I assume that the rule is implemented so that a situation won't exist where nonexistent claims are being conjured up and "sold" to attorneys, thus fostering a whole illegal scheme of creating false law suits. The legal term for this conduct is champerty.

However, as with most "one size fits all" type of situations, while the general rule of not lending money to clients is sound, there certainly are or should be exceptions.

During the time that the case was going on, and certainly during the extended time that the case was protracted due to the increasing seriousness of the injury, my client approached me several times with stories such as "I have no heat in my house, and my children are coming down with pneumonia"; "I have no electricity in my house, my children are falling down the stairs because they can not see."

I suppose you can just recite the rule of no lending money to clients and dismiss your client's plea out of hand. But, of course, it is not that easy. And you can be sure that many of your clients will be hustling you into giving them some money, and you, as an attorney, are actually happy that you can tell your client "Gee, I would like to lend you some money, but my code of conduct does not allow it."

But is the response, as here, where you know your client is seriously impaired, where the distress your client is suffering is legitimate, and where your client is in a serious position to suffer irreparable harm, to blithely say "I just can not lend you the money you need."

The truth be told, unscrupulous clients also have another arrow in their quiver! It is not unheard of for a client to take their case back from the attorney if the attorney will not give the client money. This hazard comes with the territory. The upstanding attorney will lose some of his cases, but nothing much can be done about this. However, it is times like this that you might be happy to fall back on your prohibition of not lending money.

My client had a multi-pronged plea to me. She needed money or they would turn off the heat. She needed money or they would turn off the electricity. She needed money or they would foreclose. (I was too smart for that particular crisis. I called the bank, explained the pending case settlement, lied a little as to when it would happen, and obtained an extension).

But, I did succumb to her entreaties and lent her several thousand dollars cash for her electricity and heat. The good news is that the Board of Bar Overseers would not necessarily find out about my transgression unless somebody would report me, and only my client was in a position to do that. And, of course, she was exceedingly grateful for my decision to assist her.

Back to the case. As I have said, I had become a bitter enemy to the claims adjuster. The limits of the insurance policy that I was dealing with was fifty thousand dollars. This means that the insurance company would protect and cover their insured, the owner (driver) of the vehicle who caused my client the injury to the extent of the limits of the policy, and in this case, fifty thousand dollars.

In a situation like this, if my client felt her injuries were more than fifty thousand dollars, she has the option of suing the driver of the vehicle directly. However, the recognized concept in a situation like this is that, there would not be appreciably any more money to be obtained by suing the driver directly, so someone like my client, through me, would resign themselves to just take what the insurance company was legally liable for. The theory is if the person who caused you damage really had something to protect, they would do so by the increased insurance coverage.

The damage to the wrist became established, and it was not going to get better. Surprisingly, the bitterness between the adjuster and me remained. I, in turn, decided that I was not going to accept anything less than the policy limits of fifty thousand dollars.

All controversies have to come to an end, and the insurance company reluctantly offered us the policy, which, of course, we accepted. There actually was other available sources of money, and, in total, I obtained sixty two thousand dollars in total for my client.

Obviously, the money coming in to me does not automatically go to my client. Accounts have to be settled, outstanding medical bills have to be paid, and perhaps some unmentionables have to be addressed. I also have to take my legal fee!

The money finally comes to me and I had to pay all the bills. There was payment for medical bills not covered by insurances; I was instructed to pay over fifteen thousand dollars in back mortgage payments; I was instructed to pay somebody five thousand dollars for a loan that they made to my client; I still had to pay the gas and electric company over and above the monies I was going to take back for reimbursement of the money that I lent her; and of course I was going to take my fee of one third of the settlement. After all, this is what I work for.

When the smoke cleared, my client received a check for a little less than ten thousand dollars.

All well and good. I made payments as I was instructed, gave my client her share, closed the file and looked for new horizons to conquer.

Several months later, my client calls and demands that I furnish to her an accounting of the total settlement, something I had already done when I originally received the money.

Fair enough. I put together a spread sheet, showed her all the checks that I paid off at her request, showed her the fee that I took, reminded her of the money that I lent her, and accounted for all the money that had come in to within twenty dollars of the sixty two thousand dollars.

Case closed, or so I thought. Several months later, another attorney contacts me, and says her client, my ex client, is seeking an accounting. Usually, an attorney will extend professional courtesy and not try and hassle a fellow attorney, if he or she can help it. This attorney took that tack. Even though our Canon of Ethics demand an attorney turn in another attorney for an obvious violation of the ethical rules, most attorneys will give their brothers (what we call each other) the benefit of the doubt, and try and work with the attorney, if possible.

I furnished this new attorney with my accounting (it was easy, I already had done it for my client directly) and now hoped that this would satisfy my ex-client.

It was not to be. My client, apparently greatly unsatisfied with my several accountings, not to mention my personal handling of her finances, and certainly oblivious to the service extended to her in lending her money, strolled into the Board of Bar Overseers and said "My lawyer settled my case for fifty thousand dollars and I did not see a penny of it."

Well, of course, the Board would have to investigate such an allegation. And investigate they did. I had to produce yet another accounting, of which I was becoming quite proficient. Unfortunately, there was no way I could hide the fact that I had lent my client money!

I did satisfy the Board that I had distributed all the money according to the liens and instructions that were given to me. This, of course, was the far more important factor of this fiasco (at least from my point of view). However, I now was going to have to be disciplined for my infraction of lending my client money. The level of distress and danger of my client's situation just could not or would not be considered in mitigating or justifying my action.

The punishment was a public reprimand and a warning not to do it again. No one wants their reputation impaired, so the public reprimand, while gently embarrassing to me, and the beginning of my own "rap sheet", was not necessarily fatal to my legal career.

On the other hand, you just can't say enough about my grateful client!

The Doctor

Background:

In many instances a lawsuit may require an "expert witness" to supply testimony regarding the topic at hand.

While it is true that many lawsuits will not have need of an expert witness, a surprising number will have the necessity of clarifying and explaining a complex situation. In a multitude of situations, your suit might have needed the benefit of an expert, but you could not have afforded to hire one.

Imagine you were to get in a car accident, where the fault was not immediately clear. An expert could give superior testimony that the angle of impact between two vehicles could only have been by car A entering the intersection before car B, thus establishing your position and proving you right. Or you could go it alone and try and convince a judge or jury that you were in the right. Obviously, if money were no object, it would always be right to have that expert

There are experts for everything.

Art experts can testify to the quality of paintings, construction experts on the quality of the house builder, real estate pros on the value of a property taken by eminent domain. As you can see, the list is almost endless.

Attorney Richard Weiss

Let me tell you something about the achievement of becoming an expert. An expert becomes one accepted by the court by being qualified by his attorney before he is allowed to testify. He will be qualified by his credentials. These credentials will be his education in the subject matter, his advanced education in the precise subject matter of this particular discipline and his experience in the field He will even be given the benefit of being an expert by the previous number of times he has testified as an expert.

The very interesting thing about an expert is he can say anything he wants to about the subject matter before him. After all, he is the expert. A layperson is quite limited to giving his opinion as the court will characterize that testimony as "speculation", and the court will just not allow speculative opinions to be presented. The court is very picky on this point. But the expert, he is the resident God, and he can give HIS opinion, because he is supposedly all knowing (on that subject). Sometimes, his opinion can border on ridiculous, but the court system allows the expert that latitude. If he has been qualified as an expert, the court can not contradict his musings and opinions. (However, a judge or a jury can choose not to believe the expert). Of course, if the expert increasingly becomes more bizarre, he may lose his standing as an expert.

A young Polish fellow comes to my office for guidance. He has just come to America from the old country, and has met up with his elderly aunt, who has been in Boston, in the North End, for several decades.

The elderly aunt was a spinster. She had worked at menial jobs all her life. However, she religiously had saved her money, and purchased several buildings, multi-family residences, at the right time.

She was living in the North End in a multifamily unit. The building was quite rundown, but still had great value as Boston entered the boom decades of the eighties and nineties.

This woman also owned a multi-family in Quincy, Mass., and she wanted to give it to her nephew.

The nephew's relationship with his aunt was probably a bit forced, given the reward at the end of the rainbow.   Unfortunately, it would seem that is often the case where someone has little family involvement. Or perhaps she knew exactly what she was doing given the non-interest of her core family.

Did the nephew use "undue influence" in convincing the aunt to give him the property? Perhaps. (This is not allowed in law). But on the other hand, who else was there for her to give it to, if not to her blood nephew, who was at least showing some interest in her.

It was my job to protect the nephew and the conveyance to him as best as could be done under the circumstances.

I looked in the yellow pages and sought out a doctor that I thought would be reasonable.

We make a date to visit the doctor soon after the aunt conveyed the property to the nephew. I, the nephew, and aunt descend on the doctor's office and I explained that we needed an assessment and evaluation of the aunt to prove that she was of sound mind at the time of the conveyance. This evaluation would be to ward off any future attacks of disgruntled relatives that might come and want to contest the transaction.

The doctor sat with this woman for approximately two hours while he professionally evaluated her. He also videotaped the evaluation for both future proof as to the aunt's soundness of mind as well as a vehicle to refresh his memory if and when the results of this interview were needed, that might be several years into the future.

Well, the inevitable did happen. Several relatives did ultimately "find" auntie enough to want to challenge the conveyance of the home from the aunt to her nephew. Meanwhile, the aunt had deteriorated enough that she was now in a nursing home.

On the side of the relatives, they were able to secure the testimony of the nursing home doctor, and he was prepared to testify that the aunt did not know what she was doing when she conveyed the house to the nephew. This doctor was not evil or prostituting himself, but I believe he was tailoring his testimony to his clients, the other relatives of the Aunt. Luckily, I would be able to rebut his testimony not only with my doctor's own opinion of soundness of mind, but I also could use the videotape of the actual evaluation from the doctor's office. I was present at the interview and I was confident that the interview would reflect a woman who had enough of her faculties to satisfy the court that she knew what she was doing when she gave over her second house to her nephew.

I contact my doctor, and hit the jackpot – sort of. This jackpot was of the negative type, and it was a doozy. First of all, the doctor had lost the videotape. Since this woman walked in off the street, the doctor had absolutely no memory of meeting this woman or what he actually did in his professional capacity.

I am not sure I could have overcome this piece of adversity, but as in turned out, the worst news was yet to come. This doctor, since our interaction, had been charged with violating his own code of ethics by being accused of having sex with some of his own patients.

I did not think that the argument of saying "well, he certainly did not have sexual relations with my client," would hold much sway.

The judge, already hostile, (I think she was related to the judge in "Father Knows Best"), now limited the doctor's testimony even more, preventing him from testifying on matters that the judge felt coincided or intruded upon the accusations against the doctor in the area of doctor-client relationship.

My client and I, under the circumstances, folded our tents and hammered out a settlement that gave the nephew a few crumbs from the pie that was the subject matter of the action, the house in Quincy, Massachusetts.

Now examine the case from the nephew's point of view. What did he do wrong? He sought legal advice and legal protection. I did what I had to do by videotaping the interview between the doctor and the aunt. The doctor's actions were outrageous, and totally unexpected, and more importantly, unable to be rehabilitated.

Assuming I did nothing wrong (which I did not) consider the astonishing bad luck that this fellow experienced. He did all the right things. He provided companionship for his aunt; he sought out legal protection in an attempt to protect the transaction between himself and his aunt. Since I could not be attacked, the expert doctor realistically could not be held financially accountable for what he had done. It boggles the mind of the bad luck this fellow ran into to lose the lion's share of this house to the rapacious relatives of this woman.

Why We Hate Lawyers II

Background:

A man cannot serve two masters. This might be the jazzy way to define a conflict of interest. In the lawyer's ethics, a conflict of interest is one of the most important concepts that lawyers are taught to check out and abide by. The concept is simple. One cannot take on two clients if, in serving one of them, you might intrude on the rights of the other one. For instance, if you are representing two clients accused of a robbery, you will likely want to convince a jury that one client could not have done the robbery because you have a good alibi for him. Obviously then the second criminal bears the brunt of the accusation. This would be a conflict of interest, and you could only take on one of the two parties. This concept is one of the strongest caveats that a lawyer must honor.

A high-powered medical malpractice lawyer gets contacted by a friend of a friend to handle a very sophisticated and non-obvious form of medical malpractice. Because of the very connection through the friends, the lawyer had been acquainted with parties related to the case in the past. Therefore, the lawyer concluded that to take on this case might hint at a conflict of interest. The lawyer even ran the fact pattern by the overseeing legal board that made decisions in cases such as these. The opinion of the board was that it was a very close call, and warned the attorney if he took the case, he would be at risk for disciplinary action if he chose to represent this client.

The standard here is that a lawyer should not represent a client where there is conflict of interest, even further should avoid the appearance of a conflict of interest (actually, not such a bad concept to practice).

The lawyer gave it long thought, but ultimately concluded to err on the side of caution. He was a successful enough attorney that he felt he could refer the case out to a colleague. In this case, he selected a business acquaintance whom he had referred cases to, and in return, had cases referred to himself.

The lawyer informed his client of the switch, assured her she would be in excellent hands with the substitute attorney, and set up a meeting. He also drew up a fee splitting agreement with the referral lawyer. The referring lawyer would receive one third of the receiving attorney's fee. This was cheerfully agreed upon by the receiving attorney as it represented a potential huge fee for not only the referring attorney, but the receiving attorney also.

Thus the long odyssey of the medical malpractice case began with lawyer number two and his newfound client. After approximately 18 months of investigation, interviewing witnesses, legal wrangling, trial preparation, and emotional fallout, the case settled for one and one half million dollars.

Our lawyer was delighted with the result in as much as he was scheduled to receive approximately one hundred and sixty six thousand dollars. (One third of lawyer two's fee).

When our lawyer approached the trial lawyer for his rightful share, the trial lawyer refused to pony up the money! His rationale: Since the referring attorney was disqualified from representing the client under a conflict of interest theory, the trial lawyer reasoned that the same imposition spilled over to NOT RECEIVING the sharing of the available fee with the original attorney. (It was still the same conflict of interest).

There are two giant concepts to bridge here. The first concept, the theory of conflict of interest, is meant to ensure that a client's representation will not be compromised. As per my explanation at the beginning of this chapter, it reflected the fact that the law will not tolerate a client's rights being compromised. But here, the case has been concluded. The client has been ably served in that the case has been concluded, and wildly successfully. There could be no conflict of interest because its very essence has been negated. No harm will or could come to the client herself. The controversy over the fee is one level removed, and, as such, goes beyond the concern of the protection of the client.

The second concept to be broached is the fact that these two lawyers were de facto business associates and friends. Therefore, it rested squarely on the trial lawyer's shoulders that he raised the issue himself, after the successful handling of the case, only because of greed. With friends like him, you do not need too many enemies.

This left lawyer one with little recourse other than to sue lawyer two for his rightful share of the fee. This now meant a whole new, and substantial lawsuit had to be instituted with all the bells and whistles accompanying the lawsuit: discovery, depositions, motions, trips to court, memorandums. All this was done and the case was actually litigated, brought to court for a trial. The court took the position that if lawyer one had a conflict of interest with representing the client, then that conflict carried through with all dealings with that client.

The flaw in that reasoning is that a conflict of interest is supposedly applied to protect the interests of a client. No matter how remote, it the lawyer does not feel that he has the freedom to do ANYTHING to protect his client, then that would be a conflict of interest. Here the client has been magnificently served and the involvement between client and law is now nonexistent.

It is the snarky officiousness of the legal system – the judges who run the system are sometimes responsible for its poor outcomes.

The judge in this case took the position as stated above and ruled in the lawyer two's favor.

Further evidence of this legal system caveat, where educated (men and women) sometimes can not see "the forest for the trees" was confirmed by the Appeals Court, upholding this position.

This finding is a good lesson for a person who feels that they have been subjected to the most horrendous, unfair decision of all time. They are not the only one experiencing this craziness!

At the Cemetary

I write this chapter to suggest all attorneys are not pricks, as the prevalent mood in America suggests. In this case, the nice guy is me!

An older attorney, now an ex-friend, tells me he has a client that he would like me to take over. This attorney is not being altruistic, the client was quite backward, almost a social misfit.

At the point my ex-friend offers her to me, I decided to take the case not so much that I am a humanitarian, but I needed the business at that time. I agreed to meet with her.

She was a woman about sixty years old and had never been married. She never had had any money and she was a marginal person at best. I am not sure she ever had serious employment.

She entered into the realm of needing a lawyer due to the following situation. She had met a gentleman who was fifteen to twenty years her senior. This person had lost his wife in the last five years and he began to befriend, or at least keep company with, this woman.

My new client claimed that they had become engaged, and perhaps they had. I surmised that either she was lying, or perhaps fabricating this scenario. It even occurred to me that her friend had also recognized her vulnerability and indeed was nice to her in his own right and became engaged to her to please her and help her self esteem. I never did find out the actual true situation, and on many levels, it is not really important.

Well, my client's paramour passed away. He left her his whole estate, which consisted of two three-family houses. While these houses were not in great shape, they certainly represented a step up in her financial situation. However, being somewhat unsophisticated, she did not use her legacy to its best advantage. In fact, one house remained vacant while she actually lived in all three apartments of the other house.

The client's first skirmish with the law was with the family of her deceased paramour. They contested the decedent's will and suggested he must have been not of sound mind to make such a bequest to this woman, simultaneously cutting out his whole family.

But the relatives were blowing smoke and had no concrete proof as to his unsoundness of mind, and in the end, they failed. The court allowed the will and the bequest to stand.

When I first met this woman, we became enemies with each other. She didn't trust me, and could not understand why she needed me. After all, she had already prevailed over her paramour's family, and she was quite content to pad around her three units, leaving the second house vacant.

However, things started caving in on her, both literally as well as figuratively. Repairs had to be made, toilets began to get clogged, the houses were falling apart, and she had no income from either house. Housing inspection services began to come to the houses and write her up for housing code violations. The city, after continually citing her for sanitary code violations, began to issue criminal complaints against her. The city also came up with the fact that she needed fire escapes to be put on both properties as a second means of egress. This latter fact is a requirement for all dwelling units in the state, all residential units must have two means of exit.

I ended up defending her in court against these criminal complaints. She had also inherited some money from her fiancé, so she could actually make these repairs and fend off the city.

On the other hand, the judge became so mad at her that he incarcerated her for her intransigence on one of her court appearances for five hours. She wasn't even that distressed over her jailing. I don't think she knew any better.

The judge and I did not know what to do with her. She was becoming dangerously close to forfeiting her properties to the state because of her inaction.

I prevailed upon the judge to give me one more chance. I took her home.

Suddenly, my client had a change of heart. She began to trust me! She agreed to rectify the housing code violations and install fire escapes. She did not go so far as to put in tenants in her five available units, but her actions were certainly progress.

In due course, I began to pressure her to sell her houses and move into an apartment. With our newfound friendship, she began inch by inch to listen to me. We put the properties on the market, and she reluctantly began to accept offers. She was still not willing to trust me completely, but at least we were not in constant warfare.

Because she was quite needy, I now became her closest confidant. She begged me to give her my home phone number and I had the bad judgment to comply with her entreaties.

On Thanksgiving morning, I get a call from her. She wants to go to the cemetery and visit the grave of her fiancé. She had not been to the grave since he had passed away five years ago. The weather was not even clear, it was raining. She is begging me to take her, crying on the phone. I agreed!

Thanksgiving dinner for me was not until late afternoon, so I thought what harm could come to me in granting her request.

I picked her up, and we go to a gigantic Catholic cemetery in greater Boston. When we get there, I ask her where the grave is, and she gives me a row and plot number, and I set out to find her designated grave.

Of course, her reference is wrong, and I was at a loss to figure out how to find the correct grave. I could not understand the row and grave markings, and this was a very large cemetery! Because this was Thanksgiving morning, the cemetery was unmanned, and we could not ask directions where her fiancé's grave was.

We spent two hours in the rain, going up and down the row of graves, attempting, as it turned out, in vain to find her fiancé.

In fact, we never did find his grave that morning. Ultimately, we called it quits and I took her home.

By this time, my client had put her complete faith in me (as well she should). We had found a buyer for her two properties, and I found her an apartment for long-term residency.

I would like to suggest this story had a happy ending, but it did not. During this time, I had to come to understand that she had developed cataracts in both eyes, and she was slowly going blind. I intervened on her behalf and I attempted to fix her up with an ophthalmology surgeon to help her.

I did find one, and he agreed to assist her. I brought up my plan of action to her, to have cataract surgery and she had a serious panic attack. It turns out she was morbidly afraid of surgery, and certainly surgery on her eyes!

She out and out refused to have surgery, or for that matter, to cooperate in any way.

I, on the other hand, was determined that she was not going to go blind on my watch.

In response to the stress of the situation, she began to stuff herself with food. She had been borderline hypertensive, and had been told by her ophthalmologist that she could put on no more weight or she could not be eligible for the surgery. To her way of thinking this was ideal. She ate herself out of eligibility for her eye surgery.

I, in turn, would not relent. I gave my ultimatum that if she did not do the surgery, I would no longer assist her. I would abandon her, fees and all. I had already assisted her in selling the properties and moved her into an apartment.

She did not relent, and neither did I. Soon after I had ensconced her in her apartment, I parted ways with her. I severed ties and never spoke to her again. Sometimes, even the best efforts do not result in happily ever after.

The Paternity Test

Background:

Like most things in law and in life, the rules for applying for a paternity test have evolved to keep pace with technology and the advancement of society. When I first started practicing back in the 70's, the paternity test was allowed by a subjective test applied by the judge. Since there were no good tests to determine paternity biologically, paternity was then established by testimony of the parties. The woman could testify as to sexual intercourse and the man could either deny that he had sexual relations or that he did not have sexual relations around the time the woman conceived. In the 80's and 90's, genetic testing came into vogue. Depending on how much money you spent, you could determine the likelihood of a match to your genetic code. The testing on the one hand was sophisticated to be relied upon by the court, but was crude enough to have different levels of reliability. You could choose your level by how much you chose to spend. For minimum pay, you could get results that were 92% reliable, a little more, the test would be 96% reliable, for substantially more money, the results would approach ninety nine percent. Obviously, the closer to perfection meant the more money that had to be spent for the test. The certainty of DNA testing had not reached the court's doorstep.

Also, at that time, as the law evolved, it was not automatic that you would be allowed a paternity test. You would apply to the court by motion and have to plead your case to the judge that you had a right to have the paternity test and it was unconstitutional etc. etc. to deny the test. At some point, practically all of the judges took the position that you would be allowed to take the test, but again there was this transition period that some judges, being conservative in nature, denied the test and just wanted to pronounce the unfortunate fellow to be the unlucky father to the child in question.

This story takes place when the conservative judges were having a hard time granting outright genetic testing to whichever male demanded it.

A woman goes to an attorney claiming that a certain gentleman is the father of her child. The child is two years old and there have been no child support payments. The woman has been negotiating with the presumed father with little to no success. The father occasionally threw a few dollars to the woman but he was really being a prick about the whole thing and was not doing much to be a father or to be financially responsible.

The fighting turned to the court arena and the mother filed a paternity suit. In the paternity suit, she alleged all of the things that she had to do which paternity would be the time and place that the copulation occurred. The fact that she had access to the male and that they indeed did consummate their lovemaking rounded out all elements that she had to prove.

This matter had gone on for several sessions in front of the judge and the judge was attempting to adhere to the old fashioned ways of just attempting to decide through an evidentiary hearing, if necessary, that the male had to be the father to this particular offspring. The putative father himself had gone through two lawyers, not being satisfied with

Justice Examined

the aggressiveness that his lawyers were showing and trying to secure a genetic test to determine paternity (again, at this time, the sophisticated DNA testing that we know today was not available.) So, any person seeking to petition the court for a test had to choose in accordance with how much money he was willing to spend to convince the court of his non-paternity. Because a party could "buy" a test that would be only ninety two percent accurate, he always ran the risk that a judge might not accept the results as definitive enough to establish paternity. Therefore, there was sufficient pressure on the petitioners to pony up the most money and seek the test that had results at a ninety nine percent accuracy rate.

After scheduling a hearing in court with his third attorney, whom our hero deemed aggressive enough to convince the judge to authorize a test, the judge herself decided to take a different tack. It seems that while the supposed father was vigorously trying to protect his rights, no one had ever clearly explained to him how the test was conducted. It was a complete blank to him.

The judge in open court finally was fed up with the persistence of the gentleman and began to address him.

"Dear Mr. Father", the judge began, "you have been in my court several times and I am now allowing you to be granted to take the genetic test. However, I want you to know that this will be the final time in court for this issue and you will have to make your decision as to whether you want the test or not. "Do you know how the test is administered?" the judge asked.

Father: "No, your honor"

Seeing an opening, the judge almost imperceptively changed tactics. Rather than try and bully the father, she began to explain the procedure. "First you have to go to a laboratory, and a doctor will prep you. Your groin will have to be shaved and then the test is administered by a large six inch needle that will be inserted into your penis to obtain the appropriate fluids for the test to be properly conducted." "Then," the judge intoned, "after the needle has been inserted for over thirty seconds...."

At this point, our hero, after turning a shade of white, spoke up and said: "your honor, I am withdrawing my petition for a paternity test and I will acknowledge paternity to the child in question."

A Nice Story

Background:

The statute of limitations is the length of time a party has to address and prosecute his case against the presumed perpetrator of the action or the crime in question. Lengths of time vary both from the time of incident complained of and from jurisdiction to jurisdiction.

In Massachusetts, with a tort (a civil wrong like a car accident), one has three years from the date of the incident to settle and conclude the matter, or to bring a lawsuit against the responsible party. Other jurisdictions have a two-year statute of limitations for torts. Medical malpractice cases are fancy names for the negligence of a doctor, and the statute of limitations usually is the same as the tort statute. Contract actions have a longer time span, usually six years, and there are different lengths of time for different actions, including criminal actions. The well-versed television watcher may have learned that there is no statute of limitations for murder.

The statute of limitations is one of the strongest concepts in law to overturn. What I mean by this is that in lawsuits, many grey areas arise that each side is eager to fine tune and shift to their advantage. The respective attorneys plead their position to the presiding judge, long before the case is actually tried in front of a jury (or judge), and decisions are made by the judge.

Attorney Richard Weiss

Many minor issues are thus addressed, and leniency for minor indiscretions is usually allowed.

However, trying to negate the statute of limitations is nearly impossible. The law will excuse lateness and extend the statute of limitations for things such as the minority of the person wronged (the court will allow a minor the opportunity to sue for three years after the minor becomes of age) or for things like a person being incapacitated for mental defects. But short of extraordinary situations, if you miss your statute of limitations, you cannot pursue your case.

I had a client in Boston who made her living by taking mentally disabled people into her home and caring for them. The job was so demanding, that in middle age, she decided to stop her job, sell her home, and move to her roots in South Carolina. Timing in life is everything. One decision that prompted my friend to make such a move was the burst of real estate prices over the last two decades. Moving from high rent districts to cheaper locales, the mover usually makes a good financial windfall through the differential in real estate prices. Places such as Boston had real estate prices go through the roof. South Carolina's real estate gains were much more modest.

During this time, a New York postal worker, sixty-five, decided to retire and move to his family's home in South Carolina.

On the trip to South Carolina, in Virginia, the postal worker's van was forced off the road by a young man who lived in Massachusetts. The postal worker's vehicle was forced down a ravine and the postal worker had to be removed from his vehicle with the "jaws of life". He was then taken to a hospital in Virginia, where he remained for three days.

He, but more importantly, his family, felt he received very poor treatment from the hospital. The hospital did do some compulsory testing, but in general, the hospital ignored him. When it was time to go, the family had to beg for a neck brace, which the hospital reluctantly agreed to. The hospital did not even provide an ambulance for the six-hour trip to the postal worker's family home in South Carolina. Twenty-four hours after the postal worker arrived in South Carolina, he became a quadriplegic.

The family, being unsophisticated in the ways of the law, naively approached several law firms to represent them in what they thought was an obvious case of medical malpractice. Much to their horror, all the law firms turned them down.

The layperson might not appreciate the difficulty and complexity for an attorney or law firm to accept any specific case, especially a medical malpractice case. There are two distinct reasons why an attorney might not accept a case, beyond the obvious reason that a lawyer just might not like the actual facts of the case (i.e. maybe the doctor actually was not negligent).

The first reason that might sway a lawyer from taking a case is that the court, in most states, has set up obstacles and safeguards in dissuading doctors and the medical profession from being sued. In Massachusetts, within sixty days of filing a lawsuit against a medical provider, the court demands that the plaintiff go before the court with a statement from a doctor stating that the plaintiff has a sufficient case to go forward. If the plaintiff does not have such a statement, the plaintiff can only go forward by placing a bond with the court to defray the cost of the doctor's defense in the amount of six thousand dollars. (This money will actually be given to the doctor to pay his legal fees if the doctor prevails in the lawsuit).

The second factor a lawyer has to weigh in whether to accept a case is the estimate of the money that the lawyer would have to lay out in preparing the case. Depending on the complexity of the case, the costs to bring a medical malpractice case to court could be fifty to a hundred thousand dollars.

The postal worker's family was running into these problems.

The family was at their wits end, but really could not figure out what to do. The family had the presence of mind to not address the case that corresponded to the auto accident where they had been forced off the road. That case could probably be prosecuted successfully, but the money available in the car accident case paled in relation to the damages that the postal worker had suffered in becoming a quadriplegic. This was so because the party who had hit the postal worker had minimum car insurance. This meant that after the forty thousand dollars of car insurance that would be paid by the insurance company, you would then have to look to the party who caused the accident, who in this case was a young student with no independent source of money to satisfy a judgment.

My friend from Massachusetts obtained a job in South Carolina with a medical facility where she would be dispatched to client's homes to assist families with significant medical problems.

She was assigned the postal family. As it was her nature, she became friendly with the family. Eventually they opened up about the obvious problem that had cast a pall on their whole way of life.

Now, on top of the medical problems, the family was under the added pressure that the statute of limitations was running. It had been about eighteen months since the incident occurred. The incident had occurred in Virginia, so the parties involved, the driver from Massachusetts, the hospital involved with the faulty care of the postal worker, and the domicile of the postal worker (New York or his destination South Carolina) gave way to the rule that the accident would be subject to the jurisdiction where the accident occurred, and consequently the laws of

Virginia would be the laws that would govern the case. Virginia's tort statute of limitations was only two years!

My former client contacted me with this fact pattern, keeping in mind that I am licensed to practice only in Massachusetts. Nevertheless, I listened to the story, and I had a hard time figuring out why this was not a good case, given the fact that the postal worker had become a quadriplegic.

I do tend to be more optimistic than most. I agreed to try and help the postal worker out, perhaps not clearly considering just how difficult a task this might be.

I had to beat the statute of limitations, but first I had to get ammunition to entice a Virginia or South Carolina law firm to take the case.

To do this, I had to generate an opinion by a medical doctor. I first had to figure out the type of doctor who had committed the malpractice, and then hire an expert doctor in that area to give me a medical opinion that would point to the undeniable malpractice. Since it was unclear to me what type of doctor had caused the problem, I had to handle this decision very carefully.

There are "hired guns", expert doctors who will testify on behalf of whoever pays them their fee. In fairness, these experts are quite honorable, and will not prostitute themselves to give a bogus opinion.

I had to find just the right doctor to match up to the facts, and my analysis took me to a doctor in Illinois. The doctor was an emergency room doctor, as that was what I decided was the root of the problem. I decided that the pattern of neglect by the hospital began with the cavalier attitude in the emergency room. Of course, the doctor's opinion could not be generated immediately. I had to supply the doctor with all the medicals, and it was going to take him several months to generate his opinion. He did ultimately come up with a favorable opinion, but now it was becoming dangerously close to the two-year statute of limitations. Time was running out, and I had to keep my attention focused on the next step.

My next task was to find a law firm that would represent the postal worker. I also knew that the postal worker had tried to employ various law firms, but just was not able to.

I belong to a network that allows me to contact an attorney in any city in the United States. This gives me an "in" when I cold call an attorney. The receiving attorneys benefit with extra cases, so by and large they are receptive to accommodate their out of state "brother".

I started my quest by contacting the representative attorney in Virginia. He shot me down, but gave me another name to contact. I followed that lead, but the attorney begged off, but gave me yet another name. This went on for fifteen to twenty contacts. No one wanted to embroil themselves in such a complicated case, and I was near the end of my rope.

Then one day, an amazing thing happened. My legwork at least had made me known to the attorneys in the area. I received a call from an elderly attorney who I dubbed as my Southern Gentleman. He had me relay the facts to him, and wonder of wonders, he agreed to accept the case.

By this time, there were only several weeks to go before the two-year statute of limitations would expire, but I now had my southern hero in tow. He assured me he had things under control.

It took him up to two days before the statute ran, but he just did file the lawsuit on time. For the lawyer to file the lawsuit, it is relative easy for him to draft a complaint. As long as he was willing to accept the case, he did not necessarily even need to see my experts report pronouncing negligence or investigate more than just take my word for it.

Second hurdle accomplished. Thereafter, for the next ten months, there was little action by my new hero, but I could hardly criticize him.

Then he called me with a bombshell. My southern gentleman, sixty-eight years old, had liver cancer, and it was terminal. However, he assured me that he would hand off the case to a colleague of his.

I panicked. I realized that the reason he might have accepted the case in the first place could have been for many reasons, all not conducive to having yet another lawyer accept the case. My southern gentleman could have been winding down his practice, and decided that he had the time and expertise to take on one more serious case. Perhaps he knew of his condition when he accepted the case, and actually felt he was doing my clients a favor by accepting their representation. (Which of course, he was doing a favor far beyond even what he might have imagined).

In any event, I now realized why he had not done that much with the case in the ten months that he had it. He probably just was not able to energetically function.

My luck and my clients' luck held up when my southern gentlemen's acquaintance agreed to evaluate the case.

Several weeks later, the new attorney contacted me and agreed to accept the case! Perhaps he accepted the case as a tribute to his friend. I never asked.

His handling of the case was dynamic. He tidied up the loose ends, made a fee arrangement with my clients as well as myself (which my southern gentleman never had done) and began preparing our case.

This second gentleman was (is) a skilled attorney and spent over seventy thousand dollars in the preparation of the case. I was always kept in the loop as to the progress of the case and gave my input on various issues.

Attorney Richard Weiss

This lawyer was an expert. He did everything that had to be done. He engaged multiple doctors to give opinions on each facet of the postal worker's treatment. He performed a "day in the life" of the victim where you go to the victim's home and actually follow him around for a day with a videotape crew to make a movie to present to a jury. If the party is seriously hurt, as this man was, the jury gets to see the futility that has taken over a person's daily routine. Certainly being a quadriplegic is a terrible sentence to endure.

Virginia has put a cap on medical malpractice cases of one million six hundred and fifty thousand(1,650,000.00) dollars. Professional preparation pays off! With some negotiation, our lawyer accepted an offer of one and a half million dollars.

While there is no minimizing the magnificence of this lawyers' expertise, you have to marvel at all the people from all the states that fell into place and allowed this action to be laid at the feet of our expert attorney, and allow it to come to fruition.

WHAT'S IN A NAME

Years ago, before modern technology ruled America, milk was delivered in some cities by horse and wagon.

As you can imagine, the horses used to haul the wagons were hardly a model of youth and robustness. At that time, you could say that the job was the equivalent of the thoroughbred racing's old age home.

The owner of a milk company had just hired an immigrant to make the rounds of the milk route. The good news was that American merchants were willing to employ people of ethnic diversity for jobs (albeit the non-glamorous job of delivering milk in the wee hours of the morning). The bad news was that there was still a touch of bias and racism that made relations between employer and employee if not oppressive, at least a bit strained.

This particular owner had just hired a new person who had only been on the job for approximately one month. On this particular day, during the morning run, the horse had simply dropped dead.

This obviously caused some consternation with the delivery person. However, he kept his wits and flagged down a policeman to let him know what happened.

A report was written up, and it made its way to the owner. When the owner received the report, all hell broke loose. It seems that the route of this milk wagon was to go down Kosciuszko Street. The report stated that the horse and wagon was found on Everett St. (To fill in the blanks, Thaddeus Kosciuszko was a famous Polish statesman and military man).

The owner saw red. All he could conclude was that his worker was up to no good. He must have been stealing the horse. It was on a street that wasn't on the milk route!

The owner insisted that the authorities prosecute the poor man. The authorities in turn dragged their feet. But the owner was relentless. The authorities had no choice but to accuse and indict.

This was in the days before mandatory public defenders. The poor immigrant had to pony up what was to him a King's ransom to be defended.

The structure of a criminal complaint is first the person has to be arraigned. This is a formal act in court that just clearly states what the person has been charged with. The arraignment is done by reading in open court the salient elements of the crime that the person is being accused of. The second meeting in court is a pretrial conference. Issues are narrowed and the government and the party try to work out a settlement, if possible.

At the second meeting, possible settlements or compromises are attempted to be hammered out. For this case, a compromise was impossible. All compromises began with the accused admitting wrongdoing. The immigrant stood fast. He adamantly stated he did nothing wrong, and was on his route when the horse just dropped dead.

By the immigrant adopting what seemed to be an intransigent position (sometimes an accused will accept a little bit more of the allegation of what he was supposed to have done in order to make a compromise), this left nowhere to go but to have a trial.

The next and final step was that of trial. A situation like this hardly ever went to trial. One way or another, the case was usually settled,

Justice Examined

even if the accused caved in. The prosecutor would usually be lenient, and everybody would move on to their next predicament. But here, the trial was inevitable.

The trial started, and the police officer was first to testify.

Prosecutor: "You were the first police officer on the scene?"
Officer: "Yes"
Prosecutor: "And what did you see?"
Officer: "The horse was crumpled up, still attached to the milk wagon"
Prosecutor: "And where was the horse and wagon?"
Officer: "Oh – Oh – Oh"
Prosecutor: "You were the officer first on the scene?"
Officer: "yes"
Prosecutor: "and the horse was dead?"
Officer: "Yes"
Prosecutor: "And the horse was on Everett St".
Officer: "Ah – Ah – Ah – Ah"
Prosecutor: "Officer, what is the matter?"
Officer: "The horse wasn't exactly on Everett St."
Prosecutor: "He wasn't"
Officer: "No, he was on Kosciuszko Street"
Prosecutor: "What do you mean he was on Kosciuszko"? Your report said he was on Everett St.
Officer: "I know"
Prosecutor: "Well why did your report say you found him on Everett St."
Officer: "I couldn't spell Kosciuszko Street."

The Bill

Two old legal warhorses had a love-hate relationship, mostly hate. This had been going on since their law school days, where they were classmates and rivals. While they had a grudging respect for each other's abilities, they never missed a chance to badmouth or take advantage of the other one.

After falling out of touch for several years, one day the first attorney learned that the second attorney had become gravely ill. He was in the hospital and was not expected to leave the hospital alive.

Upon hearing this choice bit of news, the first lawyer dictates a bill addressed to the office of the second attorney.

"For services rendered, research various cases FIVE THOUSAND DOLLARS." This bill is mailed immediately to the second attorney.

The first attorney actually forgets about his letter and several weeks go by.

He gets a call from the second attorney: "What's the meaning of this bill you son of a bitch. In forty years you've never done one thing for me. How dare you send me a bill like this?

First Attorney: Oh I see you survived your hospitalization.
Second Attorney: Damn right I did. I ought to …….
First Attorney: Ignore the bill

A Gift from God

Background:

Res Ipsa Loquiter. In our training in law, we borrow many phrases from the Latin. This particular phrase means the thing (act) speaks for itself. It is a concept that is allowed to be used when there is an obvious wrong done by a person (negligence) but it is just too hard to prove. The most common example to illustrate the concept is that a car is parked at the top of a hill and rolls down the hill, injuring somebody. The hurt party cannot prove the brake was not properly set, which would have caused the injury. The concept of res ipsa loquiter allows the victim to sue the owner of the vehicle on the theory that the act could not have been anything else except the person did not set his brake. That omission of care (not setting the brake properly) is by far and away the most likely cause of the car rolling down the hill, causing injury.

As you can well imagine, res ipsa loquiter is a legal concept that is only allowed grudgingly by the courts. The courts do not like speculation and this theory comes perilously close to speculation, so the courts allow it quite guardedly.

A mother and father come to me with an auto accident that occurred to their child. Their child was only seven years old at the time, which unfortunately would portend trouble in the future. The child had gone out into the street and was hit by an oncoming car. His damages had been serious, but not permanent. He did have to have a minor skin graft from his hip to the front of his body. This was serious enough to make the case worth at least five figures.

When I first spoke to the child, he was able to sketch enough of his actions as well as the car that struck him that we would be able to put on a "prima facie case". (A case that contains all the legal elements necessary to prove the case). However, it was close between satisfying the concept of a prima facie case and not being able to sustain our burden of saying enough to implicate the wrongdoer, the driver of the car. I warned the parents of this possibility, but English, not being their first language, made anything that I said always having the chance that my clients might not understand. I now believe they did not fully understand the penalty for not putting on a prima facie case but this is such a subtlety, that even sophisticated English speaking people might get confused.

I prepared the case quite well. Because of the way the child sustained his injuries, I felt I needed an accident reconstructionist to verify that the injuries that the boy suffered were caused by the impact of the boy with the automobile.

I remember almost wrestling with my expert on the living room floor in order to assist him in understanding the way the child could have sustained the injuries given the respective angles of the boy and the direction the auto was traveling.

The other side did not meet my demands for settlement, so we were forced to take the case to trial. The day arrived and we all converged on the court, the victim, his parents, my expert, and the other side. A judge always tries to settle matters, and he took us into his chambers to have a "settlement discussion". When the judge heard the facts, he put enough pressure on the driver of the auto to offer us fifteen thousand dollars. Things were looking up.

You always have to take any offer you get to your client, and I now had a lot to talk about with my people.

When I approached them, I informed them of the offer and took a few minutes with my now nine-year-old victim. Much to my horror, when I wanted to go over the facts of the accident, my now nine year old wanted to take the low road and stated he remembered nothing about the accident. I reminded him that he had previously given a fairly comprehensive and logical account of the accident. This did not sway him. Whether it was that he had lied previously, or the trauma of the accident had made him forget, or he was just nine years old, he held firm on his position that he could not remember anything about the accident.

I now hastily convened a meeting with his parents. I told the parents we were in real trouble. If their child could not lay out the very basic facts of the accident, we could not establish our "prima facie case". If we could not do that, we were in dire danger of losing the case. You see, the penalty for not putting your case in properly is not a slap on the wrist. If things are done wrong, or if all the procedure is not just so (All elements of a tort case have to be satisfied) the other side can move to have the case dismissed. Even if a case is obvious, if you do not have a person to recite the very basic facts to your prima facie case, you will not be allowed to go forward. Since I had not crafted my case with "res ipsa loquiter", I was not prepared to get my case in by that route.

Unfortunately, while my clients were not very educated or sophisticated, they had been exposed to the concept of res ipsa loquiter, so they were relatively complacent in taking the position that they were not in any danger of losing the case because the case was "obvious", how else could their child have been hurt if not for the negligence of the driver?

A little knowledge can be dangerous. I told my clients that I did not think res ipsa loquiter applied and we were in real danger of now losing this case.

I perhaps couched our position in a way that angered my clients, because I put the onus of this change of events on their son.

This position upset the parents and they equated what I was saying as a slur against their child.

"Our child is a gift from God", was what I had to contend with. "He is perfect, a good boy".

It is unfortunate that we are not more trained in addressing life-challenging decisions. We experience such monumental decisions as to who we will choose for a mate, what house we will buy, and now even what means of transportation we will choose. Most of these decisions we sneak up on. They are not done at the drop of a hat and they may be carefully researched. (A ten-year engagement). Sometimes, a decision may have to be made at the drop of a hat, but those situations are rare.

If that is the case, your choice of decision can be critical and perhaps life changing. It might be unfair, but it will be instantaneous, and you may not get a chance to recover from your decision.

My clients faced such a crisis. Perhaps fifteen thousand would not be life changing, but it was a good chunk of change.

I pleaded with my clients that under the circumstances, fifteen thousand dollars was fair. I even magnanimously agreed to waive being reimbursed for my expenses, which were substantial (but not my fee!).

Nothing I could say would sway them. I could imagine them losing out on ten thousand dollars (their share). This was not the first time a decision like this had arisen in my practice, and the outcome usually had disastrous results.

My clients forced a trial. True to his word, the boy testified that he did not remember anything and the judge duly decided I had not put in my prima facie case. He decided against us.

My client's parents never batted an eyelash, at least not that I witnessed.

Perhaps God made up the difference.

Wedding Night

Background:

In America, when people marry, the wife may assume the husband's surname, but does not necessarily have to. What is never addressed, is whether the wife, upon divorce, MUST give up her married name. In the absence of fraud, the answer in no. A wife may retain her married name.

Many years ago a thirty-year-old electrician contacts my office for representation for a divorce. I make a date to meet with him and to discuss the facts of the case.

It seems he found a young lady who had worked at a large corporation, and consequently had built up a significant pension plan with her employer. The parties agreed that she would stop working upon marriage and he would be the breadwinner with his electrician's license. Therefore, she would, and did, cash in her pension and this became the sole significant asset of the marriage.

Also this particular gentleman was of Slavic descent, and he had one of those difficult Middle European surnames (perhaps not to another Slav!). Upon discussing the divorce, my client, while mildly interested in his share of the pension proceeds, was adamant that the wife should not be allowed to keep his surname as her official last name. He felt he had a proud and close-knit family, and she had not "earned" the right to use his name.

Alas, I told him he really did not have much say in whether he could block his soon to be ex-wife from using his name. That was just the way the law was written.

I tried to negotiate with the other side. They blamed the demise of the marriage on my client and felt he had no claim to any of the pension money. They did not even consider my client's request for her to abandon her married name.

In a case like this, while all assets come under the jurisdiction of the court, a judge would tend to give the lion's share of the assets to the party who brought the assets into the marriage, if he considered the marriage short term (five years or less) which this marriage was.

My client had not informed me of any unusual facts of the marriage that I should know or be wary of.

As we girded up for a trial, my client warmed to the fact that he was entitled to half of the pension assets – and still demanded for his wife not to use the family name.

The trial begins, and the wife is the first to testify. The questioning went something like this:

Attorney: "What is your name and address?"
Wife: "Mrs. X"
Attorney: "Were you married to Mr. X?"
Wife: "Yes"
Attorney: "How long had you known him before you were married?"
Wife: "Two years"
Attorney: "At any time did you move in with him and live together?"
Wife: "No"
Attorney: "At any time before marriage did you engage in sexual relations with him?"
Wife: "Yes"

Justice Examined

Attorney: "For approximately how long did you have relations with him prior to the marriage?"
Wife: "Approximately one year."
Then, the bombshell.
Attorney: "Did you have sexual relations with your husband after you married?"
Wife: "No!"
Attorney: "Did you have sexual relations on your wedding night with your husband?"
Wife: "No!"
Attorney: "Are you telling this court that you never had sexual relations with the Defendant after you were married?"
Wife: "That is correct."
Attorney: "Did you ever ask your husband why he would not have sex with you?"
Wife: "He would not discuss it."
Attorney: "Did you want to have sex with your Husband?"
Wife: "Of course."

I looked at my client and shrugged my shoulders as if to say, "give me something here to fight this statement." I received nothing! He looked straight ahead and gestured to me to do the same. Good enough for premarital sex, but too impure to be his wife!

Needless to say the trial did not go well from there. The wife was awarded most of the pension funds, and by the way, she kept his name.

At the Gaming Tables

I am sure that most people who have come in contact with or frequent casinos have learned the hard way that gambling at casinos is a losing proposition.

There perhaps are two exceptions to this statement. Poker players do not really "bet" against the casino, but fight it out with other poker players. Therefore, a superior player would be able to win, even while playing in a casino.

A second exception to being a guaranteed underdog at casino play is playing the game of Blackjack. The reason one can win at casino Blackjack is because Blackjack is a "finite" game. What this means is that because when you play you utilize cards from a deck of cards (or several decks), then the odds slightly change by the cards actually used in previous deals. The flow of cards, coupled with a sophisticated strategy as to how to play certain card combinations, allows players to actually have a slight edge AGAINST the casino.

This phenomenon is well-known by casinos and gamblers alike, and it affords a few very talented and sophisticated players an edge over the casino.

An acquaintance of mine was such a counter and bragged that he was ahead of the game to the tune of 1.1 million dollars. This gentleman had been playing Blackjack against the casinos for over twenty years.

Attorney Richard Weiss

Because he was such a frequent (and successful) player, the casinos try to limit the play of successful "counters" as the professional Blackjack players are known. The more successful you are, the more well-known you become, and the more hassled you become.

My friend finds himself in Las Vegas for a vacation/Blackjack excursion. Before he knows it, he is down fifty thousand dollars. At this point, he makes a decision that between the stress of the game, and it being increasingly tough for him to play unfettered, he would call this trip his last hurrah. In his somewhat agitated state, he decides that he will take a real shot to make big money, but if he loses, he concocts his last ditch plan. He decides that if he loses substantially, he will be able to negotiate his losses, perhaps at fifty cents on the dollar.

Well, he gambled all day and all night, in what I am sure was a self-induced fog.

His results: four hundred thousand dollars in the hole. Big shooters such as he are usually able to get casino credit and this gentleman leaves Las Vegas owing the aforementioned four hundred thousand dollars.

Back home in Massachusetts, this gentleman begins his campaign to negotiate and reduce his indebtedness. Unfortunately, he runs into a giant roadblock! It seems that the same people he beat out of 1.1 million dollars, and the same people who paid him every last cent of this 1.1 million want him to pay them back dollar for dollar of the four hundred thousand that he now owes back to them.

This unexpected snag in the negotiations sets my friend back a bit. Since he was unable to negotiate fifty cents on the dollar, negotiations broke down.

My friend lost interest in addressing this problem, and in turn, in the short term, Las Vegas left him alone.

Unfortunately, he developed a sense of freedom in this dilemma, and he did not do the problem justice by just ignoring it.

On a weekend, a Saturday morning, a band of constables, sheriffs and lawyers alight at his home armed with warrants for his arrest, with the indebtedness stated at the four hundred thousand dollars.

The Las Vegans had planned their ambush beautifully. Because it was Saturday morning, the courts were not open and my friend obviously could not post the four hundred thousand dollar bail that they were seeking. My friend was arrested and put in jail for the whole weekend.

For a white collar person with no criminal record, being in jail for the weekend was quite a sobering experience. To tell you the truth, he was scared shitless.

Monday morning finally rolls around and my friend is taken before a judge at one of our district courts.

Presentations were made, and arguments were made on behalf of the casinos, and of course, on behalf of my friend. The judge, after absorbing all the arguments, sort of gave my friend the home field discount of setting bail at five thousand dollars. Frankly, I feel this was as much of a criticism of the out-of-state high handed actions and timing of the day of the arrest (Saturday) as the amount of bail they were seeking.

The above is phase one of the story. My friend still had to now deal with the criminal matter as well as the practical matter of addressing the payment of the four hundred thousand indebtedness.

My friend now comes to me with this problem and (finally) asks my advice. I inform him that I am acquainted with perhaps if not the best known and respected attorney in Boston, this lawyer was probably the most popular attorney in Boston. Not only that, his expertise lay in gambling related matters. This dilemma was right up his alley.

I had met this lawyer years before because he needed an expert in pari-mutuel wagering. Pari-mutuel wagering is the system of how

Attorney Richard Weiss

bets are processed at horse and dog tracks. I was actually hired by this gentleman to be his expert where he was defending Wonderland dog track, at the time the largest dog track in the country. We won!

My friend contacted this attorney and made an appointment to meet with him.

At the meeting the attorney listens to my friend's story, with all the twists and turns, and especially the failed attempts at reducing the outstanding obligations to the various casinos.

The attorney tells my friend that he thinks he will be far more successful in dealing with the casinos. His fee will be one-third of what he SAVES my friend from the outstanding indebtedness.

This seems encouraging to my friend and they get set to do business. The attorney informs my friend that to be successful and to show that they mean business, it would be best if the attorney had funds on hand if he were to negotiate a deal. After all, if he beats down a casino for fifty cents on the dollar, it would be excruciating bad form to say "Okay, thank you. We will pay you fifty thousand dollars on the one hundred thousand dollar indebtedness, and we will send you that money in the next six months."

The lawyer says that part of the forgiveness on any debt would be the fact that the casino could at least get their money instantaneously.

This made sense to my friend. The attorney asked for one hundred and fifty thousand dollars, and my friend agreed to pay that amount to the attorney.

Within several weeks, my friend delivers the money to the attorney. This occurred in the winter and early spring of the year.

Several months go by and my friend would make periodic calls to the attorney. The attorney was always there to field the calls and my friend was continuously assured that the lawyer was making progress.

Summer rolled into fall and my friend's phone calls started to become unanswered.

Finally in October and November, my friend made concerted efforts to see the attorney as rumors of all types of malfeasance began to swirl around.

In December, the shit hit the fan. This famous attorney, who had the bearing of your wife's pudgy uncle, stood accused of stealing seventeen million dollars of his client's funds. Buried in that amount was my friend's what now seemed modest one hundred fifty thousand dollars.

My friend was still to suffer an additional indignity or two. The law firm had a five million dollar policy that this act of embezzlement fell under. Yet, the policy was written in such a way that the insurance company, while "defending" the firm in this enormously complex situation, was allowed to charge its attorney fees against the five million dollar policy.

You can imagine how much might be left after the insurance attorneys charged the five million dollar coverage for their work.

All of this must be some type of cautionary tale to stay on the straight and narrow.

Why We Hate Judges

Background:

Cashing in on one's insurance coverage can become an elaborate affair when one actually has to turn to the insurance company for financial protection when a claim is made under the policy of his or her insurance.

The structure of having the insurance company protect you is similar in practically all situations, whether it is medical or legal malpractice, or whether it is something as mundane as an automobile accident.

If you hurt somebody while driving a car, your insurance company will step in and try and settle the claim, of course for as little money as possible, but the insurance company nevertheless is by your side protecting you. If an agreement cannot be reached, the parties (the person you wronged and your insurance company representing you) will commence a lawsuit and ultimately go to court

Sometimes it is a blurry line and a possible conflict of interest when your insurance company, who is supposed to be representing you, hires an attorney to protect your interests. The insurance company technically has no interest in the case on a personal level. That is, they are representing the insured's interests, so all decisions should be made only to benefit the insured, but such is not always the case.

Attorney Richard Weiss

An oral surgeon is asked to perform oral surgery for one of his patients. He was to pull several teeth and put crowns in the patient's mouth. While his female patient was sedated, he decided to have what he thought was harmless fun. He had some tooth related prosthetics, fangs, tusks and large teeth, and he had a merry old time of putting these devices in her mouth when she was out cold. He took pictures of his escapades and he became so enamored of his "work" that he showed the pictures to his victim.

That was the wrong thing to do. The patient sued and the oral surgeon went to his dental malpractice for protection from the suit.

The insurance company, naturally enough, declined to cover him on the theory that his actions went well beyond the purpose for which the dental malpractice insurance was supposed to be used for, the inadvertent wrong actions of the dentist while he was in the midst of performing his job description, treating people for oral dental problems.

The victim sued her dentist, and won a judgment for two hundred thousand dollars. The judgment, however, had to be satisfied by the surgeon himself, as the insurance company refused to honor his demand that they protect him under his contract of insurance.

That would have been the end of it but the surgeon was not quite done. He then sued his malpractice carrier for essentially breaching the insurance contract between the insurance company and himself, the doctor. He accused the insurance company of abandoning him and their obligation to defend him under his contract of insurance.

You would think that this a cut and dry issue. I certainly do. How in the world could any person in jurisprudence actually construe that the doctor's action fell under any conceivable mantle that would suggest that the surgeon's actions were proper and were in the insurance description of a dentist performing his work.

Justice Examined

And if by any bizarre quirk, a learned judge might actually think that the surgeon should have been afforded protection, the appeal court covers for that irrationality by having a panel of judges decide appeal cases. In this case, there were nine appeal judges that rendered the following decision.

"Inserting the frivolous prosthetics conceivably fell within the (insurance) policy's broad definition of the practice of dentistry"

Really?

Let us not forget that judges are ex lawyers that may have gotten too big for their britches.

The doctor was awarded two hundred and fifty thousand dollars by the appeals court, even more money than the surgeon originally was responsible for.

Accident Prone

Backgkround:

Everyone knows that the advent of the computer can revolutionize various endeavors in surprising ways. There are many situations where governmental money payments are negotiated and paid to various recipients. These payments can range from Social Security payments, medical payments, payments made to pay obligations, and payments made in conjunction with legal settlements. A legal settlement is created where one side settles with another who has wronged them (usually in an automobile accident) but these settlements span all types of situations.

The computer has revolutionized how payments can be attached and intercepted if the recipient of such payment has outstanding obligations that are government-tracked.

Poor unfortunate scofflaws, who may owe back child support, or owe on their taxes, might find the mini bonanzas that they were looking forward to from their fender bender is rudely interrupted when Big Brother confiscates the money to pay the outstanding obligation.

Clever business people have even thought up other diverse uses to track people who are to receive unexpected windfalls or mini windfalls. Some programs track how many auto accidents an individual might be involved in. If it is excessive, the several insurance companies in any one area will be put on notice and can act accordingly.

However, the above was not always the case. Before the computer and its broad reaching tentacles there was not this interlocking web of tracking one's movements, or their participation in extraneous areas that heretofore were not tracked. As in any discipline, there are always those who will attempt to abuse the system rather than try to work within it.

A good deal of my practice is doing small automobile accidents. Prior to computer sophistication, some people learned how to play fast and loose with getting hurt in accidents.

A client of mine recommends a person who was just in an auto accident. I was eager to respond.

I meet with a middle-aged female. We sit down and she describes an accident where she was a passenger. She has all her paperwork, names of the party who hit her car, the car she was in, the hospital that she was taken to, and everything else to make the case a dream to handle (no contributory negligence issue as this person was a passenger, and a passenger can not be responsible for an accident). Contributory negligence is the concept that a party may have harmed you by causing an accident. But within the facts of that accident, you did actions that partially caused that accident to happen. For instance, a vehicle may have hit your car, but you might have been speeding. The further rule is that if you are deemed to be contributory negligent, you can still receive damages from the other party, but the damages are reduced by the percentage that the innocent party "contributed" to the accident. The "innocent party" will not receive anything if the contributory negligence exceeds fifty percent.

I asked her what her injuries were, and she answered that her right calf was injured. When she walked, there was pain. She had even started her treatment and engaged the services of a chiropractor.

As I inquired further about her injuries, she became uneasy, but was adamant that her only injury was her right calf.

I had the presence of mind to ask her if she had been in other car accidents. She began to get very uneasy and became quite evasive to my questions. Finally I said I could not take her case unless she was completely honest with me.

She responded sheepishly by saying she had been in seventeen accidents over the last two years. "And I presume you have hurt seventeen different parts of your body in these accidents," I opined.

"As a matter of fact yes, how did you know?"

"A lucky guess", I responded

I declined the case.

Close to Home

Background:

As we have discussed, statutes of limitations are among the strongest concepts in the legal world. What I mean by this is that the courts give almost unconditional deference to the statute of limitations. If a party had two years to file a paper, and the paper gets filed in two years and a day, most likely all courts will not give the party who is a day late the courtesy of filing late. The two year and one day party is simply going to be out of luck in attempting to file the paper. This is just the way the legal profession, as a whole addresses statute of limitation problems. The court is usually quite lenient with other deadlines (i.e. a court demanding a response to an opposing attorney filing papers, after the lawsuit has been filed.) But in a statute of limitations case where the crux of the problem is the initial beginning of the lawsuit by filing the paperwork, if you miss your deadline, even by a day, you are usually doomed.

While the length can vary from state to state, the statute of limitations for torts is either two or three years and the statute of limitations for contracts is usually six years.

At the beginning of my marriage, I practiced law and my wife became a Biology professor at Emmanuel College in Boston, Massachusetts. The college gave many benefits including favorable medical coverage.

Most medical coverage differentiates between family and non-family plans. Obviously, the more expensive plans are the family plans.

My wife and I did not have children right away. Since we were confident we could monitor our wild animal urges in not creating a baby, we chose the no family plan. After five years of marriage we decided the time was right to have a baby.

Emanuel College is run by the Sisters of Notre Dame. The college charter demands that the President of the College be a nun of the order of Notre Dame and there are many nuns and priests who teach at the school and run the administration.

After our decision to try for a baby, my wife dutifully went to the Administration and met with a nun who was in charge of medical benefits. She informed the nun that we would like to change to the family plan. I thought that would have been that.

In due course, I and my wife had a baby girl. Nothing seemed amiss until I received a supplemental bill for the birth of my daughter.

We were upset at the error the College made. Since I am the lawyer, my wife assigned me the task of rectifying this problem.

I requested an audience with the President of the College. She was happy to receive me. It was as if we each were ready for our first skirmish. I said my wife would not make a mistake like this. The President countered that her nun would never make a mistake like that. Tie for the first round. I asked why my wife would have had a meeting with the nun if not to change our medical coverage? She countered that there were many reasons my wife could have wanted to talk to the administrator. I won that round.

As I was arguing with her, the President became frustrated. She accused me of enjoying myself during this meeting, which I cannot say that I wasn't. The President told me that her father was an attorney, and this is the way he argued. I felt that was a compliment.

Justice Examined

We parted ways with no agreements. The President vowed that we had to pay the extra money and I vowed I would fight anything of that ilk in court. I was a little miffed that the school would not do the "right" thing and just absorb the extra money. Perhaps I am too naïve.

After the initial bills came for the birth, we did not receive any others. Of course, I ignored the original bills. I was primed to see what would happen next.

I did not expend too much energy worrying about this problem. Though, since no one dunned me, and no further bills came, there was not that much to fret about. Since the Statute of Limitations for contracts in Massachusetts is six years, I knew I was safe after my daughter celebrated her sixth birthday!

Why We Hate Lawyers III

Background:

Appeal. The appeal process is greatly misunderstood by the layperson. After a lawsuit, in most situations the losing party has the right to appeal his loss to the Appeals Court. While every person has the legal right to appeal a decision, they do not necessarily have the legal basis for an appeal.

A case is appealed when there is an error that has been committed by the presiding judge. For instance, if you wanted a person to testify at your trial, but the judge, for whatever reason decided that person could not testify – and the judge was wrong, that would be an appealable issue. Obviously there are other reasons (such as the case was decided "against the weight of evidence") but you get the idea.

Felony. If you go amongst a group of miscreants with liberal "rap" sheets, there will not be much difference between that person's misdemeanors and felonies. But an educated person, or at least a person on the cusp of respectability, desperately will not want a felony against his name. If that person has not attained his job for life, having a felony against your name is quite devastating.

A prominent attorney purchased a box of very expensive cigars for himself. They had to be shipped. He found that the additional cost for insurance for loss was only marginal, so he decided to spend the few extra dollars and insure and protect his property.

He received his cigars and slowly and lovingly smoked his cigars, and when they were gone, he basked in the knowledge that not only could he afford the best, but he smoked them in a manner fitting their lofty status.

Unfortunately, he over-thought his position and decided that insuring the cigars was a little bit of overkill, even if it was not that expensive.

He gave this long thought, and finally he came up with what he thought was a brainstorm. He would put in an insurance claim!

Many things are accomplished in their presentation. This was no exception. Our hero placed an insurance claim stating that the cigars had been lost in a series of small fires. Again, the presentation was impeccable.

The insurance company, when they figured out just what a "series of small fires" actually was, balked and would not pay the claim.

Our hero now was in the swing of things and decided to press what he considered was his advantage.

He filed a lawsuit and would not back off from the suit. He forced a trial and the trial produced a finding on behalf of the attorney for five thousand dollars.

The judge ruled that the insurance policy could have been written much better and "tighter." The judge had a heavy heart, but he felt he had to rule in the favor of the attorney. Sometimes the judge in a lawsuit is bound to construe certain situations to the letter of the law. In this case, the judge felt he was constrained to rule on the case by language found in the insurance policy. (We also have a rule in general that if there is ambiguity in a written document, then the ambiguity should be resolved AGAINST the party who drafted the document.

Justice Examined

Here, it was the insurance company's insurance policy, so any ambiguity should have been decided against the insurance company.)

The insurance company was outraged, but they mulled over their options, and decided an appeal would be too costly, and given the fact that they did actually lose the case, then an appeal might also be fruitless.

Accordingly, in due course, the insurance company issued their check for five thousand dollars and took their lumps, or so it seemed.

The attorney was ecstatic at his little escapade. He attributed his somewhat tainted gain to his sheer brilliance.

Not so fast! On the negotiation (cashing) of the check, the insurance company filed a criminal complaint for intentional arson and criminally prosecuted the attorney.

The attorney was caught off guard. He suggested the insurance company was overreacting and should not be taken seriously. It was pointed out to him that the insurance company's act was no more frivolous than his own for doing the lawsuit in the first place.

As you can well imagine, the attorney did not receive any sympathy from the state's prosecuting attorney. Our cigar attorney wanted to characterize his action as a prank; but of course, he had cashed the check he received, and had no intention of returning the proceeds.

The prosecutor, fueled by the outrage of the insurance company, actually wanted to give jail time to the attorney.

Finally, cooler heads prevailed, and the prosecutor was satisfied with no jail time, but a monetary fine of ten thousand dollars. More importantly, the prosecutor insisted that the attorney accept a guilty finding to the felony of arson. This would then be on the attorney's record for life, with whatever negative ramifications a felony conviction would carry. For instance, if the lawyer wanted to become a judge, this felony conviction would shortstop that.

All parties on the insurance company's side finally felt justice was served.

The Lottery

A potential client called and requested a consultation with me. I asked him about the nature of the problem and he informed me it has to do with the lottery.

Lottery games are now held in most states. In Massachusetts, it actually was illegal to have a lottery until approximately twenty years ago. The state had to get permission from the legislature to conduct a lottery, which it did. Before the legislature gave their permission to the state for a lottery, it was specifically outlawed by the General Laws of Massachusetts. The lottery now is wildly successful and one of the most successful lotteries in the nation.

The client arrived and we went to my conference room.

Me: "Mr. Smith, what seems to be the problem?"

Mr. Smith: "When my evening paper was delivered last night, the paper had put in a correction from the winning numbers that they had published in their morning edition. It seems the fifth number (out of six) had been listed as twenty-two in the morning, but the paper corrected their error and changed the number to twenty-nine. Imagine how I felt! I began to get cold chills and then I broke out in a sweat. My hands were trembling so badly, I could not hold my coffee. I did not get control of myself for

	three hours. I am still not in control of myself, even as we talk."
Me:	"Well, I see how this could be terribly upsetting to you. Obviously, there's a lot of money involved and you have every right to be upset. What were the wining numbers?
Mr. Smith responds:	"1 3 7 14 29 (now) and 34."
Me:	"Yes that is terribly bad luck, but I am not sure what I can do. May I see your ticket?"
Mr. Smith:	"What do you mean my ticket?"
Me:	"I just like to see the ticket and verify your numbers," I replied.
Mr. Smith:	"I don't have a ticket"
Me:	"Didn't you just tell me you had a winning ticket before they corrected one of the numbers? Isn't that why you are upset?"
Mr. Smith:	"No, my dear man. I don't even buy lottery tickets. I just felt bad for all those ticket holders who must have been disappointed when they changed the number."

Precedent

Background:

Each state has their copious written laws. Laws are made by a state's legislature, and of course, there are many situations that have to be covered. Over the years, when a new situation arises, if there is not a law to cover it, then the legislature will go to work to make one.

Even with all the laws that exist, you can imagine that there are many more situations that come to pass, that there is not any precise law that covers that EXACT situation. In many situations, the most subtle change in facts could easily sway the decision from one side to the other.

Lawyers are allowed to draw off previously decided cases to bolster their own position in a legal situation. The court recognizes these previous decided cases as governing law for the underlying set of facts that the previous case stood for. This concept is called precedent. A judge must give credence to what a previous case, with a similar set of facts, stood for. Though, as you have seen, a judge has the ultimate right to ignore other cases, or for that matter, even existing law to make what they feel is a just decision.

The cases that we consider as "precedent" are previous cases that have been appealed to the Appeals Court by the disgruntled side. When the appealed cases are decided, they are catalogued and kept as the permanent record of that state's cases. All of the other cases that are not appealed or not chronicled, never come into play. A case with similar facts that was decided against the prevailing case law never comes into consideration, for the main reason that the current combatants might not even know such a case with similar facts existed or was litigated. On the other hand, a lawyer who was privy to a decision of a case that was heard in court but not appealed (so there is no official record) could at least try to bring it to the court's attention. The judge is not bound by the decision, and probably will not want to hear of such a collateral case because he will want the freedom to use his "superior" intellect to rule on the case before him.

I represented a client who had been a little surly when having to give information on an insurance claim. However, through perseverance of the insurance company, my client finally provided all relevant details. Now, the opposing attorney (representing the insurance company) had asked that my client be defaulted for his non-cooperativeness.

I, of course, had done research and was quite confident that opposing counsel's arguments were baseless. In researching my opponent's claim, I also get to see all the law and cases that address the issues that opposing counsel raises.

We go before the judge and my opponent presents his case.

Opposing Attorney: "Your honor, in Weston V. Blackwell, the case clearly states that an insured who at any time does not cooperate with his insurance company is denied from the coverage that he is seeking".

When I hear opposing Counsel's utterances, I am flabbergasted. Not only have I never heard of the case that counsel is citing, but I know that every other case on the subject, which there are many, stand for the opposite point of view.

I am temporarily stunned and for once, the judge picks up on my body language. The judge, who had been around the block in his own right, also was familiar with this attorney. The attorney was not really evil or trying to gain a complete unfair advantage, just was comfortable in bending the rules, or in this case, actually fabricating certain facts to gain the slightest of advantages. The judge was ready for him.

Judge: "Attorney, I am not conversant with the case you cite, are you Mr. Weiss?"

Me: (a little excited) "Your Honor, I never even heard of that case."

Judge: "Where did this case come from?"

Atty.: "I can not actually recall, your Honor, I ran through so many in my research."

Judge: "I am impressed with your diligence". "However, are you regaling this court again with your made up cases and case cites?"

Atty.: "I assure you, your Honor, while the case that I cited might be suspect, the points of law that it stands for are right on point."

I won my motion.

The Flood

Two fat cat middle-aged industrialists find themselves at the pool at their Florida hotel. They lounge around drinking their pina coladas, thoroughly enjoying themselves.

After several afternoons, they notice each other and strike up a conversation. The first industrialist asks his new acquaintance how he comes to be at the hotel.

The second industrialist says he was a furniture manufacturer and he had a fire. His attorney did a marvelous job of settling his case, and he decided to "take the money and run" and just quietly retire with his business proceeds. He was enjoying his decision for his retirement.

The second industrialist puts the same question to his counterpart and the first manufacturer responds.

"My story is very similar to yours. I also was a manufacturer, of shoes, and I had a flood. My attorney also did a marvelous job for me and my settlement and I also chose to retire, rather than jump back into the business world.

There is a respectful silence and finally the second industrialist says:

"HOW DO YOU CAUSE A FLOOD?"

The Beginner

Background:

Prima facie is the concept that when you present your legal case at court, before you begin to try and overcome your opponents' denials, you must make sure that all the elements and facts of your case are laid out at court.

For instance, there are four elements in a negligence suit: a duty owed (to a person), a breach of that duty, causation (that the actual act caused your problem), and damages. If you presented a case that had the first three elements of negligence, but you suffered no damages, then you could go forward with your lawsuit, but you could not realistically win, because you would not be awarded any money.

In Massachusetts, there are six or seven grounds for divorce. Most divorces are now done on a "no fault" basis, but others do exist. A no fault divorce means that the parties feel the marriage irretrievably has broken down, that there is no reasonable chance that the parties could reconcile. The original six grounds for divorce were cruel and abusive treatment, adultery, incarceration in a prison, gross and confirmed habits of intoxication, impotency, and desertion. Before the no fault divorce, the concept was flawed because if two parties just wanted a simple divorce with no allegations of wrongdoing, they still had to adhere to one of the above six listed reasons for a divorce. Most "friendly" divorcing parties usually used the cruel and abusive ground to obtain the divorce. One of the parties, usually the wife, would have to testify that the husband abused her. Approximately thirty-five years ago, Mass rectified this situation by adding a ground of irretrievable breakdown. If both parties feel the marriage has irretrievably broken down, then the court will accept this as a legitimate basis for divorce.

Early in my career, but after I graduated from public defending, I represented a client in a divorce action. The client's husband had abandoned her and I had to file the divorce for desertion.

I operated on the theory that her husband was nowhere to be found (of course) and thought I had fulfilled all the steps to get my client her divorce.

I obtained a court date and I and my client arrived at court on the appointed date and time. My case is called and it is up to me to present my "prima facie case" to the court. We are there without the husband, and I begin my questioning. In a situation like this, it is really very easy because you do not have an adversary harassing you at every turn. But you must present a case with all the elements that constitute your case to allow the court to approve it. It was my job to plug in the prima facie case.

"Ms. Jones, has your husband abandoned you?"

"Yes"

"And when was the last time you saw him?"

"Two years ago"

"Have you seen him since?"

"No"

I look up to the judge with my best puppy dog look.

"Is that sufficient your honor?" (Translation: "Have I put in my Prima Facie Case?")

Judge: "No, inquire again"

Oh, ok. I am now not sure what I am supposed to do. I figured the only thing I Could do was ask the questions in a different manner.

"Ms. Jones are you living alone?"

"Yes"

"When was the last time you had sexual relations with your husband?"

"Two years ago"

"Have you seen him since?"

"No"

Again my begging demeanor to the judge.

"Is that okay, your honor?"

"No"

At this point, the judge thinks things over and says: "You're lucky I'm in a good mood. I know you are new. I'll help you out this time, but don't think this will ever happen again."

The judge proceeds with questioning.

"Ms. Jones, has your husband been gone from your home for more than one year?"

"Yes"

"Would you have taken him back into your home during that one year if he had asked to be taken back?"

My client thinks about this and senses that it is imperative to get this right to get her divorce (which was absolutely correct!).

"Yes your honor"

"Okay, I will grant the divorce for desertion."

"Counselor, I gave you a break today because you're new, but I won't let it happen again if you come to court unprepared."

"Thank you, your honor"

I hastily gather my paperwork and my client and exit the courtroom.

As we were leaving the courthouse I realized I would not always be the new kid on the block, but I wasn't sure I was going to be able to keep pace with the courts expectations for my performance.

The Psychic

Long before 9/11 a woman calls and asks if she could come to the office. I ask her what her problem was, but she declined to elaborate, but reiterated she definitely needed my advice.

When she came to the office, she was a middle aged woman rather exotically dressed.

"And what do I owe the pleasure of this visit?"

"I see visions," she replied

"What kind"

"I can see plane crashes" she said.

"Have you ever reported one before it happened?"

"No, that is why I came to you. I need your help to tell me who to see or how I should go about doing this."

"I'm sorry," I said. I can't really get involved with people who think they're psychics. I have my own reputation to protect."

"But you don't understand," she said. "I am a real psychic."

Public Defending

Backgkround:

New young attorneys sometimes turn to public defending when they are unable to get a job any other way.   If a new attorney does not catch on with a law firm, or does not secure an adjacent or similar position with any type of business, he might have nothing to do, even with degree in hand.

The legal world of a young new lawyer is a little like the resident system with doctors, where the medical community squeezes out several years of very hard work with long hours from a new doctor. Public defending is an opportunity for young lawyers that allows them to hone their legal skills while also being employed and actually getting paid for their troubles. There perhaps is an issue that these indigent clients get representation commensurate with what they are paying for, but then that is an issue for another time.

CWOF stands for Continued Without a Finding. A cornerstone of lawyering in criminal work at all levels, large cases and small, is the attempt of lawyers (and their respective parties) to attempt to settle the case at hand.

When a lawyer gets a "Continued Without a Finding", the court is saying that they have heard enough of the facts to determine that the party is guilty of the crime, but because either the non-severity of the crime, or the fact that this might be the perpetrator's first offense, the court is willing to grant the party mini probation, stating that upon the party staying out of trouble for a short period, maybe 3 months to a year, the court will wipe the complaint off the record of the perpetrator. In the criminal justice system, this is the Holy Grail of Public Defending.

I also applied to be a public defender in the early part of my career. I did learn more how to be an attorney, and the meager pay was much appreciated.

I was in court on my scheduled day, and a party was brought in who was a semi-regular. This person had an extensive "rap" sheet, but all his transgressions were of the minor, non-violent type. He had many driving violations, some minor robberies and disorderly conduct. His current offense was shoplifting.

As luck would have it, I was chosen to defend him. Of course, he was responsible for the offense he was allegedly accused of, but he was more than happy to "accept" a CWOF if I was able to get one.

I thought it was not going to be a problem to get a CWOF. After conferring with my new client, we approached the Assistant District Attorney, also young lawyers on the other side of the law, whose goal was the same, to hone their skills for a much higher paying job in the future, in the very near future for those who really hated the job, which I am told a lot of the Assistant District Attorney's do. On the other hand, there are many lawyers with a law and order predilection, and this job certainly allows them their chance to single handedly right the ills of society.

I contacted our ADA, and after some sophisticated negotiating, and a lot of begging, my ADA was willing to agree to present to the judge an "agreed finding of a CWOF with a probation period of one year."

Justice Examined

You are allowed to present an agreement to the court, and the court can accept or reject it. If it is rejected, you have a right to withdraw your admission (essentially that you admitted to the facts presented against you), and have a trial. It would be the ultimate decision of the judge, at a "bench" trial (trial by the judge) to decide whether you were innocent or guilty of the complained offense.

When we presented our negotiated agreement, the judge, much to my chagrin, rejected the agreement. He based his decision on the fact that the party had too many arrests and "CWOFs" and perhaps it was time for him to experience going to jail if he kept ignoring how the system worked, and kept thinking he could always get off with just a slap on the wrist, a CWOF.

I was mortified, I as yet had never represented a party that actually had done time, gone to prison for the offense that they committed. My client took this turn of events like a pro. (A career criminal pro, that is).

After going before the judge and learning that the judge was not going to accept our agreed finding, the court gave us a new court date for a trial. (When the court does not accept your "admission" to an act, you are allowed to withdraw it with no stain that you admitted the crime).

The court had to do some paperwork before they released my client, so with our new date for court, we parted ways. The court asked my client to wait in the courtroom until they did what they had to do. I departed for my office.

I was also on duty at the same court for more clients the next day, and when I arrived at court, who should I see but my new found client from yesterday. He was strolling out of the courthouse as I arrived and when he saw me he lighted up like a Christmas tree.

He rushed up to me and grabbed my hand and thanked me profusely for my representation. He also informed me that he wouldn't need my services, as all the charges against him had been dismissed.

This didn't make any sense, as the court just yesterday was hunting for his scalp.

"What happened?" I asked.

"Remember when they did not let me go yesterday, they put me in a holding cell until they could find the paper work." "And ".....I intoned. "They forgot about me! I was left alone and locked up all night and they didn't know I was even in the building." You should have seen all the red faces this morning when they discovered I was still in a cell!"

I decided I had to remember this move the next time I really needed a big concession from the court.

Running the Office I

If a lawyer does not get a job with a large law firm, and opts to still practice law, he becomes a small businessman. Whether the lawyer likes it or not, he has to manage his personnel, hire and fire associates and support staff, manage his checkbook, and do a whole host of things that must be done to run a business successfully.

One of the things I greatly dislike is interviewing prospective hires, whether it is for an associate position, or even support staff.

Firing people is even more distasteful to me. I think some people may get off on this and see it as their power trip, but I can do without it.

I had made friends with the lawyers next door. After several years, they had to break up the office, and this meant that several secretaries found themselves without a job. One of the ladies approached me and asked if she could work for me. I needed somebody at the time, and I saw no reason not to accommodate her.

She began working for me for several months, and her work wasn't great, but I am a pushover and I let this slide.

However, she kept going down hill, and I finally made the decision to let her go.

The fateful time came, and I tried to be discreet and call her into my office, and told her I decided to let her go. Much to my surprise, she laid into me with a tirade of obscenities and swear words that even made me blush. I actually was impressed, because for all her vulgarity, she did not cross over the line of any ethnic or religious slurs.

However, she surprised me even more by concluding her tirade with: "And you know what, you are as dumb as you look!"

Well you can imagine, any person would be proud as a peacock to hear a slur such as that. But what could I do. I held the power, I held the job, and I thought I was doing the fair and correct thing.

Well, you may ask yourself, could she have been correct, was I really that dumb, or for that matter, that ugly. You might think there was no real way that I might ever know.

However, in this case, fate stepped in and answered the question with emphasis. Several months later my dismissed secretary calls me, and asked if she could have her job back. And I, with my customary right on decision-making, said that she could!

I guess that definitively proved her point about the dumb part.

She did not last that long in her second tour of duty, either!

Running the Office II

I had hired a middle-aged woman as my secretary. She was unmarried and I believe that allowed her to devote all her energies to her job and serving me and my interests.

She was so devoted to me, in fact, that my other employees resented her. She was not concerned with leaving early or taking marginal days of pseudo vacations (i.e. Veterans Day, St. Patrick's Day.) In fact, if she had her druthers, she probably would have worked for me seven days a week.

The problem sometimes with people who have had a limited exposure to how to act in social situations is that they may not know how to act in obvious situations.

One day, one of my employee's hears my secretary answer the phone:

Secretary: "Oh, I am sorry sir, I can't tell you that"
Hesitation while the caller talks.
Secretary: "I will tell Mr. Weiss you called"
Hesitation
Secretary: "No sir, I can't do more than that".

My paralegal reported this conversation to me. I called my secretary into my office and asked her what the caller was asking. She responded that he was asking the address of the office.

Attorney Richard Weiss

"And why wouldn't you tell him" I asked.

"Oh, at my last job, I was never allowed to give out our address."

I didn't even bother to ask what or where she previously worked. "In this job", I screamed, "I want people to come to my office". "It is with new people, I get more work to do. We're not hiding!"

Still, she was loyal as a dog to me!

Good News/Bad News

Background:

There is a constant tug-of-war between liberal and conservative thinking. Liberals want to reform criminals, conservatives would like to put them away forever. The State of Massachusetts presently allows wrongdoers to go back into society after they have served their debt. The problem is that sometimes even after a criminal serves his time, the public gets upset if the party is let back into society, in what is perceived to some, as too soon.

A party who has earned the right to go back into society sometimes gets the right to leave earlier, but the authorities exact a price. The price is they will put that party on parole, usually with extensive "conditions."

When you are put on parole, you must sell your soul to the government by agreeing to all types of conditions the criminal system demands if they are going to let you back into society early. Obviously, most criminals will agree to almost anything for the chance of early freedom On the other hand, most criminals are not Rhodes scholars, and there might be some miscommunications and misunderstandings between the parolee and the authorities.

A career criminal, though not of the violent type, is doing time for his latest misjudgment. His parole comes up, and he readily agrees to all terms of the parole.

The obvious limitations are heaped upon the conditions of release, and our hero agrees to all of them. The only problem is that learning all of the conditions of contest might necessitate reading the papers of his parole as well as listening to further limitations verbally told to him.

Limitations such as not associating with known felons, doing drugs, getting into other criminal situations are easy, but this gentleman was also prohibited from going to restaurants where Keno was played or buying lottery tickets.

This latter prohibition is the nub of this chapter. Our hero not only purchased lottery tickets, but he had the good fortune (perhaps) of hitting a million dollar payout.

Not only did he get lucky and hit one of the big jackpots, he actually posed with lottery officials showing off his good fortune.

Obviously, if our hero knew he was not supposed to buy lottery tickets, I daresay he would not have gone out of his way to pose for a newspaper picture. More to the point, if he actually knew he was forbidden to buy lottery tickets, I am not saying he would not have purchased them, but at least he would not have flaunted his actions.

The point is it is hard to understand how an activity that is sponsored by the state be simultaneously a forbidden act to be denied the parolee. The action further speaks to the inefficiency of the criminal justice system where our hero was probably not made conversant with all terms of his parole, at least he certainly didn't understand or appreciate all the new things he was forbidden from doing.

When the powers that be learn of this parolee's violation , buying lottery tickets !, they make all types of political noise in how they have apprehended him and will decide if they will revoke his parole for this blatant violation.

In any event, the justice system, it would seem, could issue this fellow a pass by not prosecuting him for violating the terms of his parole, in the manner that he had.

Here is a fellow who probably didn't get many breaks throughout his life. The Massachusetts legal system, rather then being ashamed of the whole fiasco, could not wait to emphasize that they were going to go after him with both barrels to make sure that justice is done, that our parolee would be punished to the full extent of the law for violating the terms of his parole, for buying those invidious lottery tickets. Anyone who thinks this makes sense must be destined for a political career.

I am happy to report that for at least this case, the authorities showed a modicum of common sense. A Judge determined that the infraction was minimal and he allowed our hero to keep the proceeds – while of course closely adhering to the terms of his parole, and not being sent back to prison.

What You Don't Know

Background:

As lawsuits progress, both sides like to fine tune their position. Many decisions have to be made "on the fly" by the judge and there probably is not a specific law that covers all minor situations. Sometimes even a judge's opinion is silly.

My client, a woman around seventy, has been estranged from her sister for many years. Both sisters are widows and their elderly father rounds out the immediate family. My client's sister had a great deal of money, which my client did not care about. My client had devoted her energies to trying to bring the family together. This is not to say that my client could not use an extra infusion of money, as most people could appreciate.

Unfortunately, as family matters go, my client had not seen her sister for several months. In February, the sister died, and the family actually hid the death from my client. My client's son, a nephew of the deceased sister, came forward to administer the estate. There was no will.

The family was successful in hiding the proceedings for several months. However, the sister had left a bequest to my client, and she ultimately found out about it. Before the bequests could be distributed to the legatees, the estate as a whole had to pay state and federal taxes that were quite significant, approximately thirty three per cent of the estate.

My client only gets to learn of her sister's death because the administrator had to go into court and request that the administrator be allowed to pay the outstanding taxes by charging each legatee their proportionate share of taxes, BEFORE any distribution is made to the legatees.

Finally, I and my client are put in the loop of the estate and we get notice that we are to go into court. The estate wants to argue that no bequests be made until the taxes are paid. My client understandably would like some money immediately. We are first hearing about the death five months after it occurred.

Since the estate can calculate that the tax percentage is approximately thirty three percent, I plan to argue to the judge to allow twenty percent, certainly a modest fraction of the total bequest, be distributed to my client.

I finally get to go before the judge and plead our position. The judge attentively listens, and she verifies to herself that we indeed just recently learned of the whole proceedings, including the potential bequest.

Opposing attorney jumps up and vigorously argues that it would be premature to release any of the funds prior to paying the tax. Her argument is so convoluted that I actually lose the thread of logic that she is trying to present to the court. But she was clearly hell bent on not releasing any money to my client. I argued that it could not possibly hurt anything to release an amount of money that would still leave the balance of money much more than what was needed for taxes.

The judge carefully listened to both of us. She then took several minutes to think things over.

The judges conclusion, she states "Mr. Weiss, I am not allowing any distribution at this time. This should not bother your client, she just learned about the money anyways!"

A Restraining Order

Background:

The court has always had a mechanism for obtaining restraining orders. However, one had to go the Superior (Higher) Court to apply for one. It was somewhat difficult and costly to do.

Approximately ten years ago Massachusetts, introduced an easy way for parties in proximity to each other (i.e. by living in the same house, or at least in apartments in the same building) to apply for, and usually obtain a restraining order. They are used, as suggested above for people in proximity to each other, but a mainstay is still married people who need to avail themselves of the protection of the restraining order.

All aggrieved spouses (usually women) can rather easily apply to the court and allege that their significant other is putting their health and welfare at risk. This is all a judge needs to grant a restraining order, ordering the other party to stay away from the party at risk as well as the premises in question for any time period up to and including one year.

Also there have been some tragedies where, the party at risk (the wife) applied to the court for the protection of a restraining order. The judge did not take the wife's application seriously, only to have a corpse on their hands after a very short period of time.

Therefore, the judges almost universally err on the side of cautiousness. A judge will rather keep a person out of the house for a year then take the chance that the accused will actually attempt to do grievous bodily harm to the person seeking the restraining order.

A client of mine comes to me ready to embark on a divorce. He and his wife are both outgoing and not meek. While there has never been a physical problem between them, that is not to say that they did not stand toe to toe with each other during their inflammatory arguments over the years.

Now that discord had seeped into their relationship, their confrontations were much more frequent and their nose-to-nose confrontations were that much more menacing.

One day as they are fighting, the wife warns my client to stop yelling and cursing at her or she will have him out of the house in fifteen minutes.

As one can imagine, this only enraged my client more, and he began to verbally abuse her even more loudly and threatening.

The next day my client comes home. His wife is avoiding him, but within fifteen minutes of him coming home, the police arrive and within another fifteen minutes, my client has a fifth of his underwear and other clothing in his hands. He was out of the house in thirty minutes!

As he was leaving the house, his wife twisted the dagger by apologizing for being off the mark by fifteen minutes.

My client spent the next seven weeks in a motel, very mad, lonely, and short of clothes.

The Public Service Rule

Background:

American Law is based on English Common Law. What this means is that the basic tenets and legal concepts of the law, such as contract law and negligence, is usually governed by the law as it was developed in England.

New concepts, such as situations that did not exist from our English ancestors, obviously are addressed by laws made by contemporary lawmakers. A trucking company that did not deliver hamburger patties on time to McDonalds would be liable for consequential damages (foreseeable), that concept being clearly borrowed from English Law. A controversy for stem cell research would be governed by our new state and federal laws, as this dilemma obviously did not exist during the time of our English ancestors.

One of the basic and venerable concepts from English law was that you could not sue the Sovereign. The king was almighty and all knowing, and the court system was content to simply leave the king as unavailable, and for the most part, this concept was the law of the land. (Every so often, the Royalists themselves got frisky and accused each other of all types of infractions, and might have even executed each other, including their king. But the prohibition against suing the king applied to the common man.)

The United States originally adopted this concept. Most jurisdictions were content to not allow the common man to sue the local (or federal) government.

In Massachusetts, approximately thirty years ago, the legislature lightened up this concept a bit and allowed the common man a little latitude. Massachusetts allowed public officials to be sued if they are negligent. Obviously, the officials are "the king" and Massachusetts, on a limited basis, allows public officials to be sued up to one hundred thousand dollars if they were negligent in the performance of their job to the person that wanted to sue them.

A homeowner came to me and said he would like to add a wing to his already existing home. In my practice, I take on many things, and I assumed this would not be too difficult.

Cities and towns like to be in charge, and the simplest route to getting this done was to go to the appropriate town officials for approval.

In some situations, the homeowner might have needed a variance from the zoning board. A variance is when a person applies to the zoning board for an exception, a dispensation, if you will, to the existing rules of the town. Here we were told we could apply to the town official who was in charge of matters such as this, and see what he said.

My client obtained architectural drawings and he and I alighted on the town official.

He examined the drawings, clearly understood what my client wanted to do, and approved the addition to the house! He even took out his approval city stamp and stamped our plans as approved.

At this point, let me describe a law that is called the "Public Service" rule. It is a convoluted concept that gives great leeway to public officials. The reasoning is that the service that the public official does is usually done for the public at large (a fireman protects all the people in his jurisdiction, as a policeman would). Therefore, if this public official is performing his job for the public at large, he might not be responsible for an error that the public servant made to a specific party. It sort of takes the teeth out of our first concept of ascribing negligence to a public official. I guess if you had to further distinguish between the negligence of a party to the public service rule, the differentiation is that if say a policeman in only dealing with you specifically, comes to your house and shoots you by accident, then you could say he was directly negligent to you and you could sue him. However, if that same policeman was called to quell a disturbance at your house, he was acting for all the inhabitants of the town at large, and he was not negligent to any specific person.

Here, my client erected his addition according to his plans. After the work was done, the town, in due course, came out to inspect his work. Much to my client's amazement, the town informed him that he would have to take down what he had just erected.

The officials were singularly unimpressed with the fact that their own town official had specifically approved the plans.

My client turned to me and asked me what his recourse was. If he was forced to tear down his addition, could he at least sue the town official for negligence in approving his plans?

After some research, much to my horror, the answer was that apparently he could not. Again, I think the distinction that insulated the town official was that he was working at his job where we had to go to him as he was representing the interests of ALL the townspeople, and as such, was protected by the concept of the public service rule.

My client had to tear down his addition. He had no recourse because of the public service rule. Didn't seem fair, at all!

The Translator

Background:

Television is rife with crime shows. One of the recurring themes in these shows is a party that is held in contempt. Even in real life, the issue of contempt is a frequent one.

Our legal system is sort of modeled after the slogan "you can lead a horse to water, but you can not make him drink." The analogy is that the court system can order a person to do many things. They can order a newspaper person to reveal his source of a story, a party in a civil suit can drag a defendant into court and order him to pay a judgment that the winning side has received. Actually squeezing the money out of the losing side, or actually forcing the newspaper person to reveal his source is another matter altogether. If a party is ordered to pay the money, or if the newspaper person is ordered to reveal his source, and they refuse, the party is held in contempt. The offending party may then be held in jail until the contempt is removed. The remedy for the contempt is putting the offending side into jail. There is no torture, or flogging, or putting your hands in the offending side's pocket, all you can do is put them in jail and wait them out. A judge can also find you in contempt if you overtly violate his rules or protocol in open court.

Attorney Richard Weiss

A lawyer who has a high percentage of Spanish clients is representing one for a divorce. On this particular day, there is a motion session for husband and wife to fight over visitation of their minor children.

In situations when a translator is needed, either the party needing the translator informs the court that one will be needed, or the file itself gets marked up reflecting the need of a translator.

For today's skirmish, this piece of information had fallen through the cracks and there is no Spanish interpreter in the courthouse to assist the parties.

The attorney for the husband steps forward and states that while his Spanish is a little rough, he will assist in the hearing to translate for his client, the husband. Of course, this would be a conflict of interest, so the court has to get the assent of the other party, the wife.

The wife agrees, and the husband is put on the stand. This begins thirty minutes of the most grueling and cumbersome testimony of the husband. A question is asked, his attorney attempts to rephrase it in Spanish to his client, which is not done smoothly or quickly. Then the attorney has to listen as his client responds in Spanish, and then report to the court what the answer was – as best as he, the lawyer, can understand it.

After thirty minutes of this torture, the judge looks at the lawyer/translator and asks him when the husband's next vacation was. To the judge's amazement, the husband answers directly February 23.

The judge almost jumps out of his underwear.

"Sir, did you understand what I said?"
Father: "sure"
Judge: "You understand English?"
Father: "I speak perfect English, your honor"

Justice Examined

The judge turns to the lawyer "Mr. Lawyer, why are we conducting this little charade upon the court, wasting everybody's time, but especially mine?"

Attorney: "I thought it would be best if my client answered in his own language."

The judge did not even bother to respond. The rest of the hearing was conducted in English.

When it was over, and every body was packing up, the judge called the attorney up to the bench. "I hope you have nothing to do today, because I am locking you up and holding you in contempt for the rest of the day." You never saw a redder face than that attorney.

My Date with Osama

Background:

Many people have commented upon and written about the profound impact that 9/11 had on the United States. This is certainly true. The obvious things are cited, such as the destruction of the World Trade Center, the loss of life, and the stepped up need for security, not only at airports, but at most other serious and substantial buildings, such as Federal buildings, large office buildings, etc.

What the lay person may not realize is that this description also had a trickle down effect to many other disciplines and situations.

In Massachusetts, our landlord – tenant laws only allow a landlord to take in advance from a prospective tenant the equivalent of three months rent for the rental unit, first months rent, last month's rent, and a security deposit (money for the landlord to hold if the tenant ruins the apartment).

Most landlords will, of course, adhere to this rule. However, one landlord, who had a beautiful and highly desirable building in the proximity of Boston College, not only charged premium rent because of how nice his apartments were, but also wanted to make sure that he would not be stiffed by any tenants if they decided to break the lease. Practically all of his tenants were college students, and a high percentage of those students were from other countries.

From obscure situations can interesting things occur and cottage industries can be formed.

I one day get a call from an elderly attorney who is planning to retire. By virtue of the above landlord's predilection, he and the landlord had come up with the following scheme. To circumvent the three month law, the landlord forced out-of-state or out of country students to pay a whole year's rent, not to the landlord, which would have been illegal, but to the lawyer as an "Escrow Agent", A person that would hold the money and feed it to the landlord on a monthly basis. In this way, the landlord protected himself from being cheated out of the total contract rent.

The lawyer offered me the job and I did not see any reason not to slip into the shoes of the retiring attorney.

I began slowly, but soon I had ten to twenty students that I held their yearly rentals for the apartments in question. At my high point, I held over five hundred thousand dollars in escrow rents.

Then 9/11 occurred. All of a sudden, foreign students were not flocking to America to obtain a college education, and this was especially true with the Muslim and Arabic students.

The apartment building had carried my name as an escrow agent, but felt that they should give their prospective tenants a choice of agents. Accordingly, they had contacted a lawyer from a prestigious law firm to also be an escrow agent.

When 9/11 occurred, and before I realized that that act would trickle down to have a negative impact on my escrow agent business, I got a call from my counterpart, the other lawyer acting as an escrow agent. It seems that this lawyer was part of an international law firm with offices all over the world. In his capacity as escrow agent, he had accepted prepaid rent from a Bin Laden, a brother or half brother to Osama Bin Laden. This Bin Laden was sending his daughter to college in America, at Boston College so he needed to avail himself of the escrow agent, as all foreign students had to, who rented with this landlord.

It seems that this international law firm could not stand the heat of having a Bin Laden on their client list. Therefore, the law firm had to remove the Bin Ladens from their client roll.

The lawyer asked me if I would take over the escrow duties of this young lady. I of course, would be given the fee for assuming her as my client.

I had to think about it, but I could not see why I could not accept her as my client. (Apparently, I did not have the same international client list that the other firm had).

On the other hand, I wondered whether the Bin Ladens would have an issue with me representing their interests. I decided that that would be their problem.

I contacted the landlord and informed him I would be making the monthly rental checks. I even sent a letter to the elder Bin Laden and informed of who I was and how his daughter's account would be handled.

In several days, much to my surprise, I receive a call from Mr. Bin Laden himself (the father of the college student, not Osama). He discussed matters with me and he seemed quite sophisticated in both a personal as well as a business sense.

His daughter had been called back to Saudi Arabia after 9/11 but I still had to pay the monthly payments, which was exactly the scenario that the landlord was protecting himself against. The landlord had a duty to try and mitigate damages by re-renting the apartment, but for the rest of the year, he just was unable to. I ended up paying the total year's rent.

For his part, this Mr. Bin Laden did not even have any qualms about asking me to attack several legal problems for him.

Business can make strange bedfellows.

Attorney Richard Weiss

You have the Power – Use It Wisely

A lawyer I grew up with from our home town tells me of the following story.

When he was a young attorney, he became involved in a very bitter divorce. As happens many times because a divorce can be so personal, and if one of the attorneys views the case from his client's perspective, that attorney herself, becomes a somewhat bitter advocate for his or her client.

My friend is in the thick of this divorce, and it is as bitter as it can get. The opposing attorney himself jumped into the fray and was relentless against my friend. Because this other attorney was far more experienced, my friend felt that much more intimidated.

Nevertheless, he did not want to show his client that he was scared to death, so my friend did the best he could in keeping a brave face when he acted on behalf of his client.

My friend was miserable. He felt he was constantly harassed and he was not fully representing the interests of his client.

He trudged along as best he could. One day, depositions had to be taken. The first one was scheduled of his client's spouse, so it was scheduled to be held at the opposing attorney's office.

As usual, my friend felt a little intimidated, but felt he could get through it.

The deposition goes as well as can be expected. There was still bitterness between and among all the parties, but they were all professionals, so somehow he got through the deposition. In his haste to leave the attorney's office, he forgets his folder! He calls the lawyer and tells him he has to get his folder back. The lawyer refuses to give it to him!

Of course, had my friend been more sophisticated at the time, he would have realized that the threat of a call to the Bar Overseers would have been more than enough to force the attorney to relinquish the folder. But he just wasn't thinking straight.

Rather than be rational, he began to wish that the lawyer was dead. Not too professional but it certainly would cure many of his problems that this bully was causing him.

Two days later, the lawyer dropped dead!

Problem solved, he was able to get his folder back.

Attorney Richard Weiss

ALWAYS LOOK FOR A BARGAIN

In my practice, since approximately 1989, I have had an associate work for me. Usually, these arrangements last only up to several years, as my associates need more money, or something else comes up, like getting a better paying job or perhaps following their significant other to a new city, or even a new country.

One associate felt that she had to make more money than I was able to pay her, so she decided to go out on her own as a public defender. I have mentioned several times in this book how that works. In her case, she was going to public defend one hundred percent of the time.

My ex-associate acquires a career criminal, a person who was not ever going to be too far from the court system. In handling his various offenses, it seems that he was involved in a car accident, and he had suffered some significant injuries to his person. Since, I was the "expert" in car accidents, she decided to give me that aspect of this fellow's many problems. I was delighted to take the case, as it seemed that this gentleman had suffered significant injury in this accident.

When my ex-associate gave me the case, this fellow was still in jail. I scheduled a meeting and went to visit him. The upside of setting up a meeting in jail is that it is quite easy to find my client "in", as he was still in jail you could say that he was a captive audience.

Justice Examined

I met with my new client and he was actually quite charming. It appeared that the injuries that he suffered in the car were connected, if not directly, at lease indirectly with criminal activity that I shall explain infra. I was worried that this criminal connection might vitiate the case as there is a prohibition against collecting damages if they were connected to criminal activity. I was not sure if the facts of the case would reflect this, but I decided to cross that bridge when I came to it.

It seems that my new client and his friend decided on evening to go out trolling, for lack of a more genteel way of putting it, for oral gratification.

My client and his friend go to an area known for endeavors such as this (i.e. prostitution etc.) and spy a female that appears to be working at the oldest profession. My client gets out of the car and begins to approach the woman when he senses something isn't quite right. He panics and begins to run back to the car. Confusion reigns as his friend panics, jumps into the car and begins to back it up. In doing this the passenger door is open and bangs my client, thus causing multiple, and serious injury to him.

Of course, they do not get too far and are apprehended. I guess I was able to get money damages from the driver's insurance was because the way things went down, my client really did nothing wrong. He did not have a chance to solicit the woman, who was an undercover policewoman, and certainly he did not offer her money, which is usually the act that triggers solicitation.

Perhaps the above confusion was best for my client (and his friend) because he had planned to pay only twenty dollars for the service that he was seeking from money strewn on the floor of the front seat of the automobile. The kicker was that not only was he being incredibly cheap (or below market) for the services that he was seeking, he planned on paying the female entrepreneur that he was going to hook up with in counterfeit twenties!

I think because the car that they were using was not stolen or illegal, and it was actually properly insured, and because my client suffered serious bodily injury, and all efforts were focused on my client obtaining proper medical care quickly, that my client was not charged with anything!

I was able to obtain twenty thousand dollars for my client, the maximum amount under the driver's insurance coverage.

Seeing as my client was out on bail for his previous offenses, this adventure worked out quite well for him.

Some people have all the luck!

Piece De Resistance
Second Chance

Background:

The following I believe to by my finest accomplishment as an attorney.

The jury system is reputed to be the cornerstone of democracy. Occasionally there are studies done to eliminate the system or streamline its use. Nevertheless, the jury system survives. Therefore, it is amazing that as soon as a person is earmarked as a jurist, he or she starts a crusade to wriggle out of their obligation. The system is quite liberal in that you are allowed to postpone your assignment. In fact, you might be able to avoid serving altogether if you know the participants, lawyer or judge, you have a prejudice in relation to the trial content you are physically unable to participate, etc. In Massachusetts, the courts have streamlined the system by making the length of the jury tenure either one day or one trial. A person only has to participate one day if they are not chosen to be a jurist on that day. If they are unlucky enough to get chosen for a trial, they only have to participate for that trial, though the trial could last several days or more.

Medical and legal malpractice. Medical and legal malpractice are similar theories. Simply put, malpractice is negligence that has been committed by either a doctor or lawyer, respectively. The only twist is that when you attack a doctor or a lawyer, who presumably has been treating you for an ailment, or for that matter handling a case for you, you will actually have to win two lawsuits. With respect to a lawyer, you must win the underlying lawsuit, the action presumably your legal professional has screwed up. This in and of itself may not be so easy. Remember, your professional ostensibly was attempting to win for you, and for whatever reason, he was not able to do so. Second, you must then prove (the second case!) that your professional, your lawyer, committed negligence in not being able to win the lawsuit in the first place.

Unconscionability is the concept that a court in the state that you practice in will not uphold an agreement between parties, even if it were entered into with no coercion or ulterior factors, if the agreement itself is so one-sided and disproportionate in relation to the stakes involved in the dispute itself. For instance, if a party had a chance to win one million dollars from his opponent due to the conflict between them, then the court would cast a wary eye if a party, for any reason, accepted five thousand dollars for full settlement of his million dollar suit. This concept of unconscionability is quite extraordinary and dynamic and, as you might imagine, not usually allowed by the court. Nevertheless, the concept does exist.

I was minding my own business one evening at the dinner table when I sorted through the mail and found a jury demand for me several weeks in the future. At first, I put the obligation out of my mind, but as the fateful day snuck up on me, I began to panic. I hoped that if all else failed and I was picked for the jury, I would be bumped by one of the attorney's handling the cases. The theory stands that the attorney with the weaker case will want to bump a lawyer or a judge (or any smart person) who gets picked for the jury on the theory that that person will see the holes in the weaker case, something the attorney for the weaker case just does not need.

I traveled to the court that I was assigned to and came to settle in, where I met up with a jury pool of eighty. There were not many cases that were going to be tried that day, so I knew I also had the edge that I might not even be picked for a twelve (or fourteen) man jury. Things were looking up!

The court called the jury pool to the courtroom and ten jurors are pulled ahead of me. I am almost out of it when I am chosen juror number eleven. I am crestfallen.

The twelve jurors plus two alternatives were separated from the jury pool. The judge started addressing the jury, explaining what was going to happen and what each juror should consider if he or she feels that they can not serve on the jury. He will call up anybody who thinks they have a legitimate chance to evade jury duty and listen to his or her excuse.

I began to marshal my excuses:

1) I have a court appointment that I cannot miss (a lie).
2) I am a sole practitioner and cannot afford to let my office run without me (this is true, sort of).
3) I am prejudiced against one of the parties (I don't even know who the parties are or what the case is about)
4) I know somebody, the attorneys, the judge, the bailiff!

While I am going over my prepared excuses, I hear the judge say, "Good, then we have a jury."

What happened? While I was rummaging around with my silly ruminations, I misunderstood the judge's instructions and now I am the proud participant of this jury.

I had to recover my equanimity and resign myself to the fact that I was a member of an Essex County, Massachusetts jury.

The judge began to address the jury. He stated the good news is that he anticipated that this would be one of the shortest jury trials that he had ever presided over.

The judge began to outline the case. A landlord in the city of Lynn, Massachusetts owned a flophouse, a seedy rooming house that housed the disadvantaged, transients, and other misfits that were on the wrong side of society's accepted inhabitants.

A fire had broken out at the "hotel" and there were several parties who had been burned to varying degrees, and two people had perished in the fire.

One of the many problems of the landlord was that he had opted not to carry fire insurance on the building. It's always good to enjoy the extra money that you have by not having to pay insurance premiums. That is, until the unspeakable happens, and an accident occurs that makes you wish that you figured out that this was the one situation where you should not have scrimped to save the premiums.

The victim had been seriously enough hurt that he was in a coma in the hospital for an extended period of time. During that time, the victim's mother had found her way to a lawyer whom she ultimately employed, and in fact, was representing the victim in this proceeding.

Unfortunately, this lawyer had become disillusioned with his client for several reasons. The first bummer was because the landlord did not have insurance. From an attorney's point of view, it is probably a thousand times more inviting to be chasing a "deep pocket", an insurance company that, if you were able to get a favorable judgment, at least you are able to collect on it with relative ease. If a party, like our landlord, has opted not to have insurance, there is a good chance that it might be fruitless to go after that party personally. Even if he had money, he probably had put his assets in his wife's name, his child's name, a trust, or any of a number other ploys to make it very difficult to squeeze money out of the landlord, should there be a favorable finding.

The second reason why the victim's lawyer was not to keen on defending his client was because his client, unbeknownst to the lawyer, had sought out the landlord by himself and was shaking the landlord down – demanding that the landlord feed him money for the injuries that he had suffered.

The landlord was not born yesterday as the victim would eventually learn, as the victim was just trying to scrounge up drinking money.

However, for his part, the landlord probably saw this situation as an opportunity to make things right or at least extricate himself from his serious mistake in insurance judgment. The landlord had made one mistake with respect to this incident. He was determined not to let an opportunity to right matters (for himself) slip through his fingers.

The victim, in his simplistic way, thought he struck the mother lode in randomly contacting the landlord - coercing money from him.

The landlord had met with the victim several times and had acquiesced to payments of three to five hundred dollars each time the victim called to shake him down.

The lawyer did not know of his client's actions, and you can imagine his disillusionment when he learned of them.

Because of the above two situations, the victim's lawyer had not even seen fit to defend the victim personally. He had sent his associate, an inexperienced new attorney to try and win this trial. While I do not feel that the outcome of the trial was swayed by the inexperience of this young lawyer, it still was not right that the new lawyer was saddled with such an important trial, and with no significant preparation on the part of the attorney, to boot.

The victim had contacted the landlord five to ten times for money. Meanwhile, the landlord carefully bided his time and set out his very neatly thought out devious trap.

When what turned out to be the final request for payment, the landlord sprung his trap. He said yes, he would give the victim one more payment, but for the victim to get that payment, he was going to have to sign a release. This release, for one last payment of three to five hundred dollars (perhaps three thousand dollars in total payments) released the landlord from all future liability and obligation for the damage the fire and his rooming house had inflicted upon the victim.

The issue, then, for the jury, was to determine whether the release that was signed by the victim should be allowed to stand. In other words, the jury was to determine if the release, for any reason, should not be allowed to limit and bind the rights of the victim, even though he had purportedly and purposely signed it.

A trial can be molded in many ways by the court and the judge. In this case, the fire at the flophouse, and who was at fault for the fire, were issues for another day. This trial was all about and only about the payments made by the landlord and the release signed by the victim.

The trial began, and the terms of the trial were that only facts pertinent to the signing of the release would be revealed to the jury. All other facts and issues, such as what happened to the victim (the fire, the damages he suffered (substantial) the medical bills accrued (substantial) were ignored. The landlord's lack of insurance would not be allowed to be brought to the attention of the jury.

Jury trials are highly orchestrated events. This is why a jury trial takes so much longer than a trial in front of a judge. There is much fencing, parrying, and counter- punching when you are dealing with a jury. Either side will come up with a fact or a theory that they feel is relevant, and, of course, the other side will protest. The judge will listen to the lawyers and then manipulate and mold what the jury can hear. Usually, there are strict penalties if an attorney crosses the line and tries to sneak in a fact that has been declared out of bounds by the judge.

Time is also wasted because the jury is continually being sheltered (by taking the jury back to the jury room) from any information that the judge deems improper or extraneous.

The trial began and the landlord's attorney fairly easily established that the victim had signed the release. During the course of various people's testimony, some of the prohibited facts slipped in. We, the jury, learned that there was a fire, the victim had suffered serious injury, and that there were substantial medical bills.

A surprise fact that came out during the trial was that the victim had had his bouts with alcohol abuse.

However, all these facts were just incidental – necessary for getting a point from A to B, so that the questions or story made sense, but otherwise, the jury was painfully deprived from the background facts and the true meat of the case.

The main and substantial fact that the defense attorney did elicit had to do with the most important fact of the case, the release. The defense lawyer asked the victim whether he recognized the release. He did. The defense lawyer asked the victim if he understood what the release was saying, the victim answered affirmatively. He then asked the million-dollar question. Did the victim understand that the document he signed was limiting him for the damages he suffered in the fire to the money he was given now, three hundred dollars, plus all the money he had been given previously by the landlord to himself. In other words, the gravy train, hardly depleted as it was for the magnitude of the injuries that the victim suffered, was over, and the victim would receive no more money after this last payment and the signing of the release.

The victim answered that he did understand that!

The trial meandered a little while longer. For the most part, the landlord's attorney felt he had proven his case. The rule in any type of legal hearing is if you get what you want, don't push it. Or to put it another way, quit while you're ahead.

The victim's attorney tried to cross examine his own client and discredit his admission, but there was not much he could do. He presented no other witnesses, and soon enough, and keeping with the trial judge's promise, the trial was over in record time.

The next step was for the jury to deliberate. The judge usually chooses a "foreman" to run the jury deliberations. I felt sure I would be chosen as the foreman. Jurors fill out mini synopses stating their name, occupation and other limited information such as the jurors involvement with law enforcement, whether the jurors had any brushes with the law, and whether they harbored any serious prejudices that would exclude them from being a juror. The judge gets to review these profiles and I assumed he would choose me. I was wrong on that assumption too.

The person chosen to be the foreman took immediate control of the jury when we went to deliberate. She suggested that we all would have a say, thus allowing each juror to give their opinion on all the facts, the demeanor and assessment of the victim, and most importantly on the ultimate reason that we were there, whether the victim should be bound by his decision to sign the release for the several thousands of dollars that he had been given by the landlord over several months, or would we spare the victim and let him proceed with his case in chief, not withstanding his signing of the release.

As I have said, in spite of the best efforts of the judge to limit the facts of the case to only facts surrounding the release itself, several facts snuck in. For instance, we knew enough to know that the victim was probably an alcoholic, even though no information or testimony had been given on this point. The jury also had seen hints that the victim had suffered damage from the fire that apparently had engulfed the flophouse. But for the most part, the victim and his attorney as well as the defendant, and his attorney, had put on a very sterile and uninformative trial. Yes, he had signed the release, and yes he had been given money for the signing of the release, BUT….. Actually there was no but. That was the problem. The victim and his attorney had offered nothing in any way to suggest that the release should NOT be honored.

Nevertheless, we were there to deliberate, and we began to go around the table, stating our views as the jury foreman had set up. (Actually, she did do a pretty good job of managing).

Several of the jurors had had experience with drinking and alcoholics. The knowledgeable jurors stated that an accomplished alcoholic could actually function in society. He could drink excessively in the morning before going to work, and then more or less get through the day, perhaps with some very dicey moments, but get through nevertheless. One might be losing his train of thought, or maybe blacking out for a short period of time, vomiting, or a general paralysis of movement. But usually the alcoholic became quite adept at hiding his condition.

We also got hints of the disability that the victim had suffered in the fire, but again, these were only hints, and the way the judge had orchestrated the trial (which, of course, was his job) so that all the extraneous tidbits that we learned were just that, extraneous information that did not go to the heart of the issue, whether or not the release that the victim signed should be allowed to stand. Our alternative finding would be that for some reason, we find that we could overrule the release, and allow the victim to continue on with his main lawsuit of being compensated for the damages he sustained in the fire. The subsequent lawsuit would be exclusively against the landlord, or whomever was responsible for the fire, whomever that might turn out to be.

There may have been some defenses that the victim could have raised. However, he had not and certainly the majority of the jurors were unaware that there might have been something else that was a "saving grace" for the victim.

Ultimately, as the turn to talk of each juror went around the room, most of the jurors came back to the fact that the victim had stated that not only did he sign the release, but that HE FULLY UNDERSTOOD WHAT HE WAS DOING WHEN HE DID SIGN IT.

For the most part, the jury was intensely sympathetic with the victim. And there was certainly an indignation, and even loathing for the landlord, but the majority of the jurors came back to the fact that the victim did sign the release and he was bound by his own actions.

In a criminal trial, the jury has to find that the accused is guilty "beyond a reasonable doubt". Beyond a reasonable doubt is hard to define, but if you assigned percentages, you would probably have to feel an accused was likely to be guilty eighty to ninety percent of the time, as opposed to a civil case where the defendant, the landlord in this case, only has to be fifty one percent in the wrong, for the victim to prevail in the case. Also, in a criminal trial, the jury has to be unanimous in either finding the accused guilty or innocent. In a civil suit, like this one, only five out of six or ten out twelve jurors have to agree to come to a verdict.

Ultimately, after several hours, the jury agreed that we would have to allow the release to stand. Not everybody was happy. One or two of the jurors would not go along with our verdict, and even some of the majority (the ten, see above) had their misgivings. Nevertheless they stood fast that this is what the verdict should be.

The jury foreman notified the bailiff that we had a verdict, and we were quickly ushered back into the courtroom. Giving the verdict and having it read was anticlimactic to the jury. The judge, just as you see on television, thanked the jury for their attentiveness to the trial, their diligence, and for performing their civic duty.

At this point, the judge usually dismisses the jury and they are free to go. In this case, much to my surprise, the judge instructed the bailiff to take the jury back to the deliberation room. I had been practicing for a good number of years and was at a loss to understand what the judge was doing.

We were a "captive audience," so there was not much we could do other than to comply with the judge's directive, and back to the jury room we went.

The judge was not going to let us fester in the jury room for too long, especially since the natives were restless. The jurors finally recognized my exalted status as a lawyer and began to ask me questions on what was going on, and I was at loss to explain anything. (Nice timing).

In due course, the judge appeared, and addressed us. He said that since this was such a short trial, he thought he could bring us back to the jury room and allow us to ask any questions we might have had about the trial, and perhaps the whole process.

The jury seized the opportunity to try and learn the facts that were withheld from them. Was the victim and alcoholic? Did anybody else die or get hurt in the fire? Was this usual to actually have two trials like we had here? (The answer to that question was that the case in chief was going to be so complex with many witnesses, expert witnesses, evidence to be entered and technicalities, and that the trial that we actually had was going to be simple in its presentation, that it made sense to have two trials. Also, as happened here, if the outcome of this issue (the release) was decided as it was, then it would negate the necessity of having the main case go to trial.

Then one of the jurors asked a question that greatly troubled the judge. Assuming the plaintiff (victim) was going to win, would the case have a substantial dollar value? Since the case had a potential for a large verdict or money settlement, then would the court want to be a party to a settlement that would be so disparate as to not seem to be fair as between the parties? In this case, the medicals alone for the victim exceeded one hundred and fifty thousand dollars. There is some correlation between medicals and the damages that a victim suffers. The judge knew the basics of the case and he knew that there were significant damages. He also knew that the money that the landlord had given to the victim did not exceed five thousand dollars. At this point, the judge looked to the heavens and began to mutter unintelligible statements. He said something to the effect that if the attorney had petitioned the court (the victim's attorney) then, he, as the presiding judge would not know what he would have done by way of throwing out the whole issue of the release. I think he was saying that he – the court – was not going to be a party to such a disproportionate settlement. Even if there were not some ulterior reason, such as the victim being confused because he was in an alcoholic haze, there was a chance, under the doctrine of unconscionability, that the release could have been negated.

The catch was that this type of procedure (unconscionability) did not necessarily have to be addressed at a trial. An attorney could raise the issue by motion, usually before the trial.

But this issue was wholly on the shoulders of the victim's attorney. If the victim's attorney was not going to raise the issue, then the court was not going to go down this slippery slope. (Even this is not completely accurate. A court or a judge, if he felt so compelled that the release was a miscarriage of justice, he could have negated its outcome by an action by the court called "sua sponte." "SUA SPONTE" means on the court's own action. Sometimes the judge, or the ruling tribunal will determine that the dispensing of justice in a fair, even-handed, and

Justice Examined

acceptable way can only be accomplished by the court's intervention, even if it is not based on the original request of an attorney. The judge here obviously felt such extraordinary action was not warranted.

Trials are conducted when facts are disputed. In this case, the disputed fact would have been (among others) whether the negligence of the landlord was the cause of the damages the victim suffered.

When facts are not disputed, there may be a trial, but it is a judge who is asked to interpret the law and see how it relates to the undisputed (or agreed upon) facts. In this case, the fact that the landlord had given only five thousand dollars to the landlord was essentially undisputed. Indeed, the landlord was relying on that fact to have his release stand up.

The problem here was that the victim's attorney did not bring that motion for the court's consideration, so it did not come before the court. The judge has to draw the line at what the court should do, or whether the court by its own actions, might be doing the job of the victim's attorney, which the court should not do. Obviously, the judge decided it was improper for him to intrude so much into the victim's case.

However, as can be seen, the judge was troubled enough to act in the manner that he did when he came back to address the jury. Perhaps he felt that the victim's attorney would "wake up" and bring a belated motion (again, that may or may not have been allowed by the court). Or that we the jury would find on behalf of the victim, notwithstanding what we heard at the trial.

In any event, I was sure that this was what the judge was thinking when he was beseeching the heavens in the jury room.

The second observation that I made was that the judge was actually talking to me! Remember, while the judge did not choose me as the foreperson, he still did have my thumbnail synopsis at his disposal. I decided, for better or for worse, that the judge, in his own subtle and clandestine way, was alerting me to the injustice of this case, as he might have perceived it. It would be unthinkable for the judge to actually approach me, or anybody, for that matter, to voice his disproval of the way the victim's attorney handled the case. But surreptitiously telling me a great injustice has befallen the victim, this the judge just might attempt to do.

Perhaps I have an overactive imagination, but I was really getting into this. If I was right and the judge was really conveying a message to me, then perhaps the judge thought something could, or should be done!

But what to do? The landlord was now immune and completely free of liability or obligation for his actions in allowing a fire to damage my victim. In criminal cases, this is called double jeopardy. One cannot be tried twice for the same offense. This means if the most horrible criminal is somehow found not guilty of a crime, and even if new evidence is found to implicate that person, he cannot be found guilty of that crime. In a civil case, the term is called res judicata.

This being the case, was there a course of action to protect the rights of our victim? The answer is yes! It lies in the concept of legal malpractice.

As we have discussed, legal malpractice simply means you have a negligence action against an attorney.

Therefore, the victim still had a chance, a remedy against somebody, in this case his lawyer, to be compensated for the damage that he suffered.

Remember that in a legal malpractice suit, a plaintiff actually has to win two suits at once. The legal malpractice suit has to show that the original action against the wrongdoer could have been won. If you prove the first case, then the second case kicks in and it must be proven that the lawyer's negligence was the cause of your not winning the first case.

Justice Examined

I certainly was not impressed with the job the victim's main lawyer had done for his client.

All this was running through my head as I drove back to my office. However, the one thing I did not know was whether I could actually represent the same person whom I just ruled against as a juror. After all, I was on the jury that denied him the right to go forward in his own lawsuit. (I assumed there was some type of conflict of interest lurking there, I just wasn't sure).

My ride to my office became more and more exciting to me, but I still thought that I would not be able to represent this client, given my status.

When I got to the office, I was too excited to laboriously explain to my staff both what had happened and what I was thinking. I immediately went to the Canon of Ethics, our code of rules that governs the ethical movements of attorneys.

I poured over all the ethical constraints that a Massachusetts attorney would be subject to. To my delight, I could not find any caveats that prohibited me from representing the client in a subsequent lawsuit. The closest I came was first, a lawyer cannot engage in any action that would be a conflict of interest. In this case, one could construe a conflict of interest if I initially knew of the story of my proposed new victim, and made my decision (with the jury) on my attempt to represent him subsequently. Of course, that scenario was preposterous. I obviously did not know the victim from a hole in the wall when the trial began, and I certainly did not make my decision based on this un anticipated turn of events.

There was really no other canon that fit this situation. Somebody suggested that perhaps I could not represent my client zealously because of my previous status in his trial, but I did not feel this was so. For instance, if, in representing him at trial, I had to address the jury, I could not say "Well, at the first trial, when I was a juror in the jury room…" That would be specialized information that I had that the jury would never have the right to know. But the antidote to this was just not to ever bring up or to ever refer to anything that occurred at the first trial, especially with respect to my capacity as juror.

Therefore, after several weeks of research, soul searching, and conferring with colleagues, I made the decision that I would attempt to represent this person against his former attorney!

The only problem was that I had made no effort to contact my hoped to be client.

My first obstacle was that as a lawyer, I was not allowed to out and out solicit him as a client. That act would be a violation of my canon of ethics. Nevertheless, I had come this far and worked myself into such a frenzy about my grand scheme, that I was determined to push forward.

I went back to court and examined the folder and obtained my soon to be client's address. I wrote him a letter suggesting that it had come to my attention that he might not have been properly represented at his recent trial. Certainly, that was an ironclad correct statement. I suggested that he might want to come to my office to discuss it, all the time not mentioning what my involvement was with his case.

The gentlemen arrived at my office with an air of mistrust in his demeanor. While he might have had a reason to be indignant, he certainly had contributed to his own problems.

His first question was what and how my involvement was in this matter and I readily told him. I then tried to outline the course of events as I saw them and what my game plan would be if I pursued his case on his behalf.

He was unimpressed with the subtleties of my carefully laid out plan and not too enthusiastic with anything I had to say. I asked him if he would like for me to pursue his case. I told him it would have to be against his former lawyer, and not the landlord and this gave him pause for thought. However, he shrugged his shoulders and said he didn't care and if I wanted to do it, I could. We concluded our meeting with him signing a contingent fee agreement. This is the contract that a lawyer usually enters into in tort cases. I guess you could hardly fault my new client from getting too excited, given his first exposure to this case and its results.

As my new client was preparing to leave, I wondered what I had gotten myself into. I was going to have to file a lawsuit, pursue the equivalent of two lawsuits, (one against the landlord and one against the lawyer), and invest a sizable amount of money and time in investigation and the obtaining of experts etc. Also, I felt that I would not have any cooperation from my client. I thought to myself of the old adage, be careful what you wish for, you might just get it.

My first move was to file a lawsuit against the former attorney. I did not know what to expect by way of criticism or response or backlash. I did file the lawsuit, and perhaps there was no Big Brother to step up and say I was doing wrong so at least at first volley, I did not receive any negative feedback.

I was on my way. Between the original trial and my meeting with my client, I had learned that my client was on Social Security Disability for alcoholism. This fact became a tremendous asset for the case. His former attorney completely ignored this fact. Even though my client had stated that he understood what he was doing when he signed the release, I was not convinced this would be the final determination on this issue. I based this feeling on the fact of how sympathetic the jurors were to this man's alcoholism – even when they were not exactly sure that that was his problem.

Much to my surprise, I was able to call my client and he actually tried to cooperate with me. He admitted, somewhat sheepishly, that he had been drinking on the morning that he had signed the release. He was drunk when he signed the release but as one of the jurors had said during deliberations, he could function while drunk. More to the point, he really did understand what he was doing when he signed the release.

Intuitively, I knew that his alcoholism should not have been dismissed out of hand. In fact, given the sympathy of the jury to my client without any mention of alcoholism, we, as the jury, might have very well "given" the decision to my client by finding that the release should not be honored if we had known he was an alcoholic.

My first move was to contact Social Security Disability and obtain an official document that would contain all the testing and professional opinions of neurologists and psychiatrists concluding that my client was eligible for Social Security payments.

My next move was to hire an expert in alcohol related problems. He met with my client and interviewed him and evaluated him.

His report was encouraging. He found that the alcoholism had the effect of impairing my client's long term or ultimate decision-making process. My client, in the short run, did understand that the release that he was signing would cut off all his rights for the future. What my client did not have because of the alcoholism was the overall insight or appreciation of what he was doing with respect to his long-term rights concerning his overall wellbeing. (or to put it another way, my client woud not have turned down a chance to get a few hundred dollars for the vague expectation to possibly get substantial money in the far off future.)

My next move was to hire an attorney to be my expert. Aside from the handling of his fee for his services, this was not too difficult. Even though this fact pattern seemed obvious, unlike a medical malpractice where the error of the doctor might not be obvious to the lay person, it would seem that not bringing out the issue of alcoholism would be obvious. There was also the issue of unconscionability. This absolutely needed a expert to navigate the jury through the concept that it was the obligation of a competent attorney to at least approach the court with the possibility that the release could be declared null and void because of the disparate amount the landlord paid versus the total value of the case. Things were looking up – a little.

I now had to face what I never ever had considered to this point – whether I actually had a legitimate case against the landlord.

There was a dispute as to how the fire started. My first move was to get all the police reports. They pinpointed where the fire likely started. They had identified a "hot spot", a spot where the wiring seemed to have failed and the wiring created a tremendous hot spot against the wood that it was attached to. This hot spot then initiated the fire. The Fire Marshall could analyze this because in spite of all the wood from the hotel that burned in the fire, the wood that started the fire had the characteristics of being subjected to tremendous heat This level of this heat was so great that it was like the levels reached when creating charcoal.

I then went to the maintenance records of the city where this fire occurred. These records are kept when various artisans, in this case electricians, need to apply to the city for permission to do electrical work on a structure.

It turned out that electrical work done by electricians had not been officially logged since the forties (the fire occurred in 1991). This was a monumental step in ascribing liability to the landlord. There had been much work done to the electrical system over the years, and all of it had been done by non-licensed electricians. Having this fact on my side, when the cause of the fire at the hotel was electrical, made the liability against the landlord that much more attainable. (Any necessary electrical work would be the obligation of the landlord to perform through licensed electricians). Things were still looking up. I also hired an expert in assessing the origins of fire, and he was able to tie up the fire to faulty electrical wiring.

Consistent with not spending money on insurance, the landlord was not lavishing too much money on such incidentals as smoke detectors and fire extinguishers and proper electrical work either. I continued to be encouraged by the facts.

During the preparation of the case, which the court puts on a three year schedule, there were also skirmishes and problems that had to be met and addressed.

I had served discovery upon the defendant lawyer. This is where each side is permitted to ask questions of the other side and request the other side produce the documents that it intends to offer into evidence at a trial.

Discovery is the practical tool that lawyers use to gain additional knowledge and to understand the basic positions your opposition is going to take. That is not to say that your opponents will attempt to obfuscate their position the best that they can, all the while "answering" your questions seemingly within the rules, but sometimes you just can't hide the basic answer to a simple question like "please list all licensed electricians who have done work on your hotel in the last ten years".

However, this was not the case with my request for production of documents. The other side cannot quite play games by hiding documents that they plan to enter into evidence (or they would like to omit to give you because of their damning nature). One would be surprised at the documents one gets from the opposing side that the other side would like to destroy, but the remote chance that an attorney could be sanctioned, even criminally, sometimes does the trick of getting the documents you are entitled to). This is so because if the other side does not produce a document they would like to be used at trial, they simply will be barred from entering it at the actual trial, if the other side has not been shown the document.

My opponents had grudgingly produced a copy of a letter that our mutual client had written. This document was written by my client presumably to assist and aid his then lawyer in the handling of the case. The document was so damning that it could have been an excellent piece of evidence to show that my client really was under the influence of alcohol and his relation to reality was quite suspect.

My client had written what was his version of what had happened that fateful night of the fire. Of course, who could really say whether he was mixing up the incident of that night or attempting to convey incidents that had occurred on some other day?

The client relayed a story where a group of the inhabitants of the hotel had met in someone's room for a party. The order of the day was to bring your own liquor, which you can be sure everybody complied with. There might have been ten or twelve people in the room. The leader of this motley group, whose room it was, became agitated at some of the partygoers. He pulled out a can of paint thinner and began running around the room splashing it on the walls and the people he was irritated at. The letter did not go on to say that the person ignited the paint thinner, but given the fact that there was a terrific fire that occurred that evening, it did not take much of a stretch to hypothesize a jury deciding that the cause of the fire was this incident and not some vague theory of faulty wiring that was being espoused by some "hired gun" expert that would say anything for a paycheck.

Things had been going so well until this setback. However, all was not lost. When something like this happens, where the fact pattern is not one that the lawyer may have encountered, he should do research and see if a situation like this had been encountered before, and if so, what view did the courts take. You never can tell when some unexpected positive occurrence may wink at you.

I did do research and was very gratified to learn that there was a fair body of cases and precedent on the subject.

The courts had held in cases with similar fact patterns that a document that was being held by a defendant lawyer in a legal malpractice case was not allowed to be used against the former client IF IT DID NOT PERTAIN TO THE MALPRACTICE ASPECT OF THE DEFENDANT ATTORNEY. In other words, the previous lawyer could only use the letter written by my client if that letter was an integral part of the lawyer's perceived malpractice. (For instance, if the first lawyer did not enter a document in a trial where his now ex-client was claiming that he should have had entered the document the malpractice defendant could then use the document itself as evidence that the malpractice attorney's actions were correct, and it was for the trier of fact (the jury) to determine whether the act of not entering the document was actually malpractice.

Obviously, such was not the case here. The first lawyer was being accused of not preparing the case, not bringing it to the attention of the jury that my client was an alcoholic receiving Social Security Disability for that affliction, and not raising the issue of unconscionability to the court to negate the conducting of the first mini trial that knocked out the landlord from any liability at all.

My opposition to the entering of this letter that was quite damaging to my client should have been a slam-dunk. That is not to say that my opponents had cases that suggested almost the opposite. (Remember, in our glorious legal system, it is not unheard of for the same jurisdiction to have made rulings on each side of the issue. Nevertheless, the majority of the case law was clearly with my position!)

I brought the issue before the judge by way of motions. While the judge pondered the facts, both attorneys waited anxiously for his decision. The judge finally responded. He takes the low road by making no decision at all! He said that he would leave the problem for the trial judge at the time of trial. Let him make the monumental decision in this quagmire of a case.

Not a win, but not a loss either.

The court scheduled a case like this on a three-year calendar. I had been preparing my case for the better part of those three years, and there had been no movement or effort for the other side to offer a settlement.

As attorneys handle cases, they are trained to attempt to settle what they can. Most attorneys understand that their cases are not a constant ego trip where they must win. What the attorney must realistically try to do is minimize the exposure of their clients in any given situation.

This case is such a maverick that I could not tell where I was with it. I certainly did something no other attorney would have even considered. The trouble is, I did not have the experience to know whether any of this is viable. Therefore, with no offers, I decided to see the case through to the bitter end. Who knows, lightning might strike.

During the course of case preparation, I received a call one day from opposing counsel. We exchanged pleasantries and he finally stopped beating around the bush and said "you know, Richard, I sent my paralegal to the court the other day and she examined the original court case...."

"And?" I snappily replied

"She found the jury list and there was a Richard Weiss that served on the jury.

"Yes?" I cleverly replied

"Are you related to that person?"

"Sort of, I said."

"What do you mean, sort of?"

"I actually am that person."

My opponent was one of the top lawyers in Massachusetts. Nevertheless, this revelation took him aback. For a moment he was speechless. But he regained his composure and finished our conversation with small talk. I was sure he was planning to do some research himself to decide if I was disqualified in any way under these circumstances. I believed I had done the research, so I was relatively confident that nothing would come of this encounter. However, there was still no overture to settle. To me that was the most important thing to transpire, but I was annealed to not having the pot of gold fall in my lap. But I did judge correctly! The issue of my being a juror was never raised again!

I had experienced one piece of extraordinary good luck. Just by sheer coincidence, I picked up the Chief of Police of Lynn, Massachusetts, the city of the flophouse, who had since retired, as my client on an unrelated matter. He provided me with invaluable information concerning the fire to make sure I was going to be able to nail the landlord. (Remember, if I could not prove the landlord was responsible for the fire, then the actions of the lawyer were irrelevant.)

Three years finally came to pass and while the court usually functions in a stodgy manner, they are responsible for keeping the cases moving. The penultimate step in a lawsuit is a pretrial conference. The court forces the lawyers to actually start preparing the case for trial. They insist you meet with the judge at court and discuss all relevant matters: witnesses, length of trial, settlement talks, experts, exhibits.

Justice Examined

I received notice from the court of the hearing date, and was instructed to bring my client, and to make sure that I, the attorney, had the authority to settle the case. That seemed rather fanciful since I still had never had a settlement overture. For their part, the court hired a mediator to see if the case can be settled. This case was projected for five to ten days, and if it could be settled it would free up precious court time to address other cases not so fortunate to settle.

The pretrial conference finally came and we went to court. The court had established the meeting to be a mediation and had hired a mediator to see if he could settle the case.

We met at court. In the room sat my client, opposing counsel, the first attorney, the mediator, and me. Except we had one more person in attendance. Upon inquiry, I found out that this last person is the "money man" of the lawyer's malpractice insurance.

For the next several hours, I was subjected to the type of bombardment typically reserved for sports mediation and the like. I had to win two cases. If I was not able to prove the landlord was responsible for the fire, the case would end. I would not be able to prove the lawyer conducted the first trial irresponsibly; the release that my client signed would stand; and if nothing else worked, you would screw up the case (well that part I made up), but I was dwelling on those things. It was not something I could just dismiss out of hand.

We wound up the meeting, and much to my amazement, I was offered fifty thousand dollars. This was the absolute first time in the long odyssey of preparing this case that there has been any recognition that the other side is taking this case seriously. It had been long journey.

Nevertheless, I did not lose my cool. While I was technically suing the attorney who conducted the trial, I was really dealing with his insurance company. In this case, the lawyer was carrying one million dollars of insurance, and my eye had been on that since almost day one. (We are allowed to learn how much a party carries in insurance through discovery).

I was taken aback by that offer but I still didn't find it hard to reject the fifty thousand. If they were willing to offer fifty thousand dollars, they would be willing to offer more. The money, or the offer, was based on "damages." What inequities my client had suffered such as pain and suffering, lost ability to work, damaged property, body scarring and disfigurement, were all compensatory. I was also entitled to be reimbursed for his medical bills. My client had been in the hospital for over six weeks in a coma; he had generated over one hundred and fifty thousand dollars in medical bills. He had respiratory problems arising from the fire. While the visible part of my client (i.e. his head, his hands) seemed normal, his body had suffered much disfigurement. All in all, my case certainly had adequate damages. So, if there were settlement talks, the money should be more substantial. I think the moneyman knew the fifty thousand was not going to do it, but that's the way you negotiate or begin negotiations. Nevertheless, the session had ended, and we were no closer to settlement.

As I have previously said, my client's medical bills alone were in excess of one hundred and fifty thousand dollars. His face was intact, but his upper body had been deformed due to the damage from the fire. My client was surprisingly calm considering the offer, considering that he heretofore sold his soul for three thousand dollars cash. I guess he had matured, and perhaps was a little awed by the offer. But he followed my lead and we parted ways with the defense lawyer, the negligent lawyer, and the moneyman.

After the meeting, which was north of Boston, we had to drive back to Boston and my client asked what was next. I said the offer would probably "stay on the table" until trial. However we now had to prepare in earnest for the trial. This court mandated meeting took place in November, and we received a trial date for the following June, almost four years after I began the lawsuit. (A person has three years to do something with the incident. If the incident is not settled within three years, if the wronged party starts a suit, this stops the statute of limitations from running.)

Several months passed until early February, and I was just about going to prepare a "trial notebook" to begin getting ready for trial when my opposing counsel gave me a call. He said that the money man had been thinking things over and wondered whether their was any problem in renewing our negotiations. Opposing counsel responded by saying that it could not hurt to ask me, so there he was on the other end of the phone.

I responded by saying that I was not opposed to open up negotiations, but I didn't see what good it could do because we were so far apart. It may have been fanciful, but I still fantasized about the lawyer's million-dollar policy.

A date was established and the ground rules were set. We each would start with our opening volley as to what we would settle for. I started with one million, and they reiterated their fifty thousand dollar offer. We would retreat to our neutral corners and come back: nine hundred and fifty thousand dollars on my end, one hundred thousand on their end. This went on for sometime, and we began to get closer. As we approached the four hundred to seven hundred thousand area, our deliberations became much slower. Finally we came to a mutual figure!

To make my long story come to an end, WE SETTLED FOR FOUR HUNDRED AND SEVENTY FIVE THOUSAND DOLLARS.

From how this started, the chances that I took to do the case, the money that I had laid out to prepare the case, this truly was the highlight of my legal career.

Epilogue

Perhaps I am not a realist. But soon after I took on this case, I became obsessed with the actions of the judge who presided over the original trial.

As I said, I actually took up the cudgel of this case based on the fact that I thought the presiding judge had opted to alert me, albeit surreptitiously, that he felt that my client had received a raw deal by not being represented properly at the first trial. Not only did it turn out that the original attorney either did not know about the concept of unconscionability, but he was also too lazy and too disillusioned to spend time (waste time?) in bringing this motion before the court.

I had made the decision to take on the case only on this rather obscure legal concept. I had been pleasantly surprised that I had even a stronger cause of action (legal way to win) by emphasizing and playing up the fact that that my client was an alcoholic, received Social Security Disability for his alcohol affliction, and this whole scenario was withheld from the jury in the first trial.

The judge would have been privy to and known the total situation. I was convinced he did in fact want to convey the situation that this client had been poorly represented by his attorney. Of course, it would have been in violation of all of our canons of ethics for the judge to become proactive on behalf of the lay victim. I am sure this would have been almost the highest form of judicial misconduct. But the judge certainly could have tried to communicate with me in the manner that I thought he did.

I had to know!

I thought it would be easy. However, I found out the judge had retired from the bench, and from practicing law, soon after this trial. There was a central clearing house for addresses and phone numbers, and I found a listing where the judge had retired to the western part of Massachusetts. It was a several hour drive. I was not prepared to go and try and meet him personally, but I did phone him.

"Judge X, my name is Richard Weiss. Do you remember me?"

Judge X: "No"

Me: "I had a trial with you about four years ago, Smith v. Jones, Do you remember that?"

Judge X: "No, I can't say that I do."

Me: "Well you said it was the shortest Superior Court Trial that you ever presided over. Ring a bell?"

Judge X: "Vaguely, what happened"?

I took a few minutes to lay the foundation. The judge said it was coming back to him. He began to remember the players, the lawyers, the outcome and the brevity of the whole thing. Most judges keep a notebook where they write down the important happenings at a trial. They put in entries, notes to themselves about things that might come up to instruct the jury etc. The judge had kept all of his notebooks! He went and found the right one. The judge looks into the notebook, but for the life of him (he professes) he can't figure out who I am.

Judge: "What did you have to do with that trial?"

Me: "I was a juror"

Judge: "Oh, What did you want to know"?

Me: "Judge, I took the losing victim as my client and sued his original lawyer for legal malpractice in not conducting that trial properly."

Judge: "Really?"

Me: "I won four hundred and seventy five thousand dollars for my client."

Judge: "That's impressive"

Me: "Judge, I just had to ask you. You took the jury back to the jury pool room and answered questions for us after the trial. Did you secretly want to let me know that the victim had been misrepresented and that was the reason you took us back to the jury room?

I would like to say he confirmed that that is what he did and he reveled in the fact that we were sort of co-conspirators in this soap opera, and he was pleased with what he had accomplished. But that is fiction and this was real life. Also, even if it were true, the judge was not going to get all warm and fuzzy and admit to a total stranger (not withstanding that I would have been his chosen one) that he violated his lawyer's canon of ethics.

Alas, he denied all such mischief and became weary of talking with me.

He bid me good-bye, and it ended just like that!

I still think I was right!

Me: "Judge, I took the losing victim as my client and sued his original lawyer for legal malpractice in not conducting that trial properly."

Judge: "Really?"

Me: "I won four hundred and seventy five thousand dollars for my client."

Judge: "That's impressive"

Me: "Judge, I just had to ask you. You took the jury back to the jury pool room and answered questions for us after the trial. Did you secretly want to let me know that the victim had been misrepresented and that was the reason you took us back to the jury room?

I would like to say he confirmed that that is what he did and he reveled in the fact that we were sort of co-conspirators in this soap opera, and he was pleased with what he had accomplished. But that is fiction and this was real life. Also, even if it were true, the judge was not going to get all warm and fuzzy and admit to a total stranger (not withstanding that I would have been his chosen one) that he violated his lawyer's canon of ethics.

Alas, he denied all such mischief and became weary of talking with me.

He bid me good-bye, and it ended just like that!

I still think I was right!

CPSIA information can be obtained at www.ICGtesting.com
Printed in the USA
LVOW13s2203160614

390340LV00001B/228/P